Have you ever wondere  *wounded? Is God really d cover reported? Stephen contrary. As a boy grow time in American history, God's fingerprints were on Stephen's life from the beginning. In direct opposition to the demonic secularism of our age, Stephen's story shows how God works in and through the life of a modern human in a post-modern era.*

Aaron Gordon
Pastor, Hillcrest Church
Monroeville, Pennsylvania

Reading a memoir by someone who knows himself well illuminates not only the writer's life but also that of the reader. Stephen Hiemstra has taken a remarkable path through life, and his memoir, CALLED ALONG THE WAY: A SPIRITUAL MEMOIR, *provides that experience. Many times as I read his work I paused to reflect on how I faced similar choices as I grew and matured. Stephen's memoir is especially rich because of the progression he made from his youth to his overseas experiences, his hard-won PhD in economics, and his career as an agricultural economist and then a financial economist, and finally his seminary training. That arc of time reveals how experiences at each stage of Stephen's life prepared him for his calling to the ministry. The memoir invites each reader to consider the span of our lives and how circumstances, events, our predispositions and inclinations have led us to become who we are today.*

Thomas H. Stanton
Attorney and Author
Johns Hopkins University

In CALLED ALONG THE WAY, *Stephen Hiemstra gives us a glimpse into his journey from boyhood to manhood. He shares fond childhood memories, daring youthful escapades, unpleasant workplace experiences, as well as satisfying accomplishments. A man whose faith was integral to his life, he reveals the promptings of the Holy Spirit that led him to a second career as a minister. It's a satisfying story that is still playing out.*

Stephen C. Gabriel
Economist and Author
Farm Credit Administration

Stephen's book, CALLED ALONG THE WAY, *shares his life through a variety of interesting experiences. Stephen has spent time in the Washington metro area, Iowa, Michigan, New York, Puerto Rico and Germany. Raised as a Christian, he worked as an economist for many years. Then, in his 50's, influenced by his sister and daughter, he was called to become a pastor.*

Karen Hiemstra Reed
Boca Raton, Florida

An interesting book that friends, family, peers and anyone who has ever met Stephen would enjoy. It is a story of the twists and turns and accomplishments of one man, in whose life we can glimpse our own.

Ben and Colleen Stewart
Niagara Falls, Ontario, Canada

Many of us go through life unaware of what it means, adding one experience after another as the years pile up. The Greek philosopher Socrates, after choosing death rather than exile from Athens or silence put this danger plainly: "The unexamined life is not worth living."

Occasionally we have examples of lives measured with care. One example is a memoir written by a man who declares on his calling card his identity as "Slave of Christ." With such a bold declaration of faith Stephen Hiemstra shares his life in Called Along the Way.

Stephen takes us through his life, sharing illustrations from his youth growing up in a religious family, his student days, his life as an economist, and his pathway to become minister of the gospel.

Stephen's book shares the struggles and joys of life helping each of us to reflect for ourselves along the way.

Rev. Dr. John E. Hiemstra
West Nyack, New York

Stephen shares snippets from his life to illustrate how he was called to the ministry. The twists and turns of his life will be familiar to those who have started their journey in one direction, only to find themselves at a different point years later.

Sarah Hamaker
Author
Fairfax, Virginia

It was a joy to hear from my friend Stephen Hiemstra after so many years who worked as a fellow economist for the Economic Research Service (ERS) at U.S. Department of Agriculture (USDA), undertaking analysis for the federal government. As a young man, he listened well, was sensitive to the needs of others, and approached his assignments with skill and enthusiasm, uncommon even among PhD economists. Even editors knew that his publications required minimal editing,

I was not surprised to hear that he has devoted his senior years to ministry or that he had become a writer. Like Stephen, I left economics to pursue a career in photography.

Marshall H. Cohen
Photographer and Author of
Denmark: A Photographer's Odyssey

Assiduously writing one's memoirs or publishing a series of letters had long been a tradition for distinguished people, giving insight to their character to family, friends, and others who were affected by their lives. Doing so also provided such authors opportunities to reflect on their lives, prepare for mortality, make peace with God, and link themselves to future generations.

As the modern age of mechanical reproduction, and postmodern age of digital stimuli, have descended upon us, this esteemed tradition has fallen into abeyance. Instead, we live in an age of nihilism, characterized by, to paraphrase the philosopher Friedrich Nietzsche, as one where many communicate as with a sentence taken out of a paragraph with no reference to the text of the page on which it is written much less the book in which it is contained. When tweeting has replaced context, it is then refreshing to read about the life of someone I have known since our days together at ERS over thirty years ago.

Stephen's life starts out as a series of dreams, punctuated by conscious choices made from God's grace at extending free will to all of us. But, we are reminded of an underlying sense of evocative surrealism throughout Stephen's book that Christ's spiritual force is there with us and within us, opening doors and pointing the ways for us to choose to enter, after periods of reflection and discernment on the trials and tribulations of our lives.

Stephen writes that in this new, highly-subjective world, "if words have no fixed meaning that we can all agree on, the potential for manipulation becomes enormous" in the absence of God's protection, especially if we do not do our homework. Books like this, especially about and/or by people we know personally give one pause to reflect on the direction of one's own life, something not done often enough in the postmodern world.

Dale Leuck
Economist
U.S. Department of Agriculture

Dr. Hiemstra's memoir captures his walk through life and his walk with the Lord that emerged along the way. His scriptural allusions help recount the major seasons of his life, guiding the reader and helping focus on the thesis and humanity of his work. His writing makes you feel as if you are watching his life unfold first-hand, even during his first glimpse of life as an innocent five-year old. Reading as been a joy.

Jessica Hiemstra
Teacher and Tutor in Math, Science, & Music.
Centreville, Virginia

CALLED ALONG THE WAY is a beautiful mix of poetry and prose that nudges the reader onward on a quest to understand the person behind the poetry; the man behind the prose. Each chapter is an experience that weaves the story of the writer through life phases until coming face to face with the almighty God. Funny at times; at others, mystifying and intriguing, Hiemstra opens up his life story for us to delve into, investigate, and learn from. It provides an excellent inside view of how God uses every facet of our lives to mold us and to use us for His glory.

Nohemi Zerbi
Chemical Engineer and Commissioned Lay Pastor
Faith Evangelical Presbyterian Church
Kingstown, Virginia

Our stories, when told, often become windows through which God's reveals his fingerprints in our lives. Such is the case of Stephen Hiemstra's story as it is told in his work, Called Along the Way. As you read it, you will not only come to understand his journey but become aware of the presence of God's hand and grace in your own pilgrimage. This discovery is well worth the read.

J. Robin Bromhead
Senior Pastor
Centreville Presbyterian Church
Centreville, Virginia

Stephen's spiritual journey is interesting because it has taken place along the pathway of enormous changes in America.

Jonathan Jenkins
Pastor, Kingerstown Lutheran Parish
Klingerstown, Pennsylvania

Also by Stephen W. Hiemstra:

A Christian Guide to Spirituality

Una Guía Cristiana a la Espiritualidad

Life in Tension

CONTENTS

Elementary School

PART 2: NEVER ALONE

Junior and Senior High School

College

Cornell University

Michigan State University

PART 3: LIFE TOGETHER

Washington Aggie

Early Married Life

Wake Up Call

PART 4: FULLY PRESENT

Journey to Seminary

CALLED ALONG
THE WAY

Stephen and Maryam Hiemstra, November 24, 1984.
Lewinsville Presbyterian Church, McLean, Virginia
Marshall H. Cohen, Photography

CALLED ALONG THE WAY

A Spiritual Memoir

Stephen W. Hiemstra

T2Pneuma Publishers LLC
Centreville, Virginia

CALLED ALONG THE WAY: A Spiritual Memoir

T2Pneuma Publishers LLC
P.O. Box 230564, Centreville, Virginia 20120
www.T2Pneuma.com

Names: Hiemstra, Stephen W., author.
Title: Called along the way: a spiritual memoir / Stephen W. Hiemstra.
Description: Includes bibliographical references | Centreville, VA: T2Pneuma Publishers LLC, 2017.
Identifiers: ISBN 978-1-942199-25-0 (pbk.) | 978-1-942199-29-8 (Kindle) | 978-1-942199-17-5 (epub) | LCCN 2016920697
Subjects: LCSH Hiemstra, Stephen W. | Clergy—Biography. | Vocation, Ecclesiastical. | Christian biography. | Christian life. | BISAC BIOGRAPHY & AUTOBIOGRAPHY / Personal Memoirs | BIOGRAPHY & AUTOBIOGRAPHY / Religious.
Classification: LCC BR1725.H458 2017 | DDC 280/.4/0924—dc23

All Scripture quotations, unless otherwise indicated, are taken from The Holy Bible, English Standard Version, Copyright © 2000; 2001 by Crossway Bibles, a division of Good News Publishers. Used by permission. All rights reserved.

The front cover image shows a linoleum block print by Allen Bjorkman (www.ReplicaPrints.com) and is used with permission. The image comes from a woodcut called a *Nauis Socialis Mechanicorum* (*Social Ship of Mechanics*) attributed to the artist Albrecht Dürer. This image also appears as an illustration in the book *Stultifera Navis* (*Ship of Fools*) by Sebastian Brant, published by Johann Bergmann in Basel, Switzerland in 1498.

I would like to thank my editors, especially Diane Sheya Higgins and Sarah Hamaker.

Wedding photograph by Marshall H. Cohen, used with permission.

Cover design by SWH.

Traveling Partners

Early Ministry

PREFACE

*D*uring my tenure as camp counselor, one memory stands out: I helped two special needs Boy Scouts, Elmer and Freddy, pass their swim test. Both had previously mastered the mechanics of swimming; I merely assisted them in overcoming emotional obstacles that hindered their progress.

Elmer swam the American crawl in perfect form, but only in shallow water where his fingers touched the bottom. When I prodded him to venture into deeper water, he became violently upset because in his heart of hearts he believed swimming was a scam.

Freddie swam fine, but he loved being rescued by the lifeguard. He typically swam a lap or two in his swim test; then, a big smile came on his face as he pretended to drown. I still remember the horror on the faces of those watching me as I shouted at this kid, until he gave up his pretense, forgot about himself, and finished his swim test.

Aren't we just like these two scouts when we hear God's call? Swim in deeper spiritual waters? Who me, Lord? Stop focusing on myself and step out for Christ? Who me, Lord? I think the hounds of heaven have been after me all my life. Yet, the chaos of life frequently cloaked my awareness of God's daily presence.

The cloak lifted one Sunday morning as my mind drifted during a long sermon in Spanish. I prayed to God: why did you bring me here? I have no Hispanic heritage or special language ability, and I try the patience of all who hear me preach. Why am I here?

God reminded me of the testimony of Nicky Cruz, whose story led me to faith in the film, *The Cross and the Switchblade*, who now appeared obviously Puerto Rican to my adult eyes and ears. This revelation surprised me because, at age thirteen when I answered the altar call, I had never met a Puerto Rican—to me, Nicky Cruz was just another New York gang member. In view of this revelation, if I am a fool for the Lord, I have been a fool since God called me to faith.

In his 1937 book, *The Kingdom of God in America,* Richard Niebuhr observed that all attempts to interpret the past are indirect attempts to understand the present and the future. If as Simon Chan (1998) writes our spirituality is lived belief, then examining how we have lived should reveal the theology of our hearts and minds (Jam 2:18–24). In this memoir, I explore my past, not only to understand how I came to faith, but also to inform my call into pastoral ministry.

It is misleading to assume that faith comes naturally or that a call to ministry proceeds directly from an idyllic life. My life experience supports neither assumption. During the later years of my government career, these verses hung on my office wall in front of me:

> But now thus says the LORD, he who created you, O Jacob, he who formed you, O Israel: Fear not, for I have redeemed you; I have called you by name, you are mine. When you pass through the waters, I will be with you; and through the rivers, they shall not overwhelm you; when you walk through fire you shall not be burned, and the flame shall not consume you. For I am the LORD your God, the Holy One of Israel, your Savior. (Isa 43:1–3)

Much like God called the Nation of Israel out of slavery to human masters, he calls us now out of slavery to shameful desires and sin. In this way, he blesses us so that we can bless others (Gen 12:3). Ministry is such a blessing.

In *Called Along the Way* I describe my faith journey from unbeliever to believer (part 1), from cultural Christian to active disciple (part 2), from disciple to awareness of call (part 3), and from seminary to early ministry (part 4). Unlike Adam and Eve, my story does not begin the Garden of Eden. If you too have struggled with your faith walk, then my story may offer solace.

Please join me.

*A*s a child, a dream returned to me over and over where I felt suspended, neither awake or asleep, but paralyzed as if lost in time and place. Everything was fuzzy: neither light nor dark, hot nor cold, silent nor voiced. My limbs had a tingly feeling, like an arm that had fallen asleep or a leg that refused to support your weight. To describe it as a dream suggests that I might wake up, but this dream lingered refusing me the opportunity to stir, as if I faced a decision. Yet, what decision?

PART I: AWAKENING

FORMATIVE YEARS

Iowa Snow

Snow is for jumping in and for making into balls and throwing.

"*Mom, why do I need a jumpsuit, a knit cap, and mittens?*"

"*Because the porch is cold and it is colder outside,*" my mother answered as she zipped me up.

"*But Mom, I don't like mittens. Why can't I wear gloves like you and Dad?*"

"*Your grandmother made these mittens and gave them to you to keep you warm while your father is in Korea. See—she attached them together with a string so that you won't lose them. When you get older, we will get you some gloves—but gloves are made from leather and you can't use them to make snowballs without ruining them. So for now, you need to use mittens!*"

"*Mom, I can put my shoes on myself! . . .*"

Pammel Court, Ames, Iowa

*T*ran, ran, ran—Mom was in the other room and the door was open—so I ran, ran, ran.

I ran around the buildings and in the alleys between corrugated huts where I played many times. Around and around I ran.

I found an open door and in I ran. A bulletin board stood in front of the counter and pool tables were everywhere. There in the Pammel Court community center, my mother found me and picked me up.

Ever Present

*T*ime awake never ends in a continuous present with no to-morrow and no yesterday. Every waking hour my mother is present with me when I am sick in California.

Happiness means having friends and not being alone. In the daytime suffering from asthma, loneliness sneaks up on me when I look out over the bed covers. Waiting. Breathing the warm mist from the vaporizer.

What is wrong with me? I thought.

After my father plays his classical music in the evening, the alligator under my bed comes out and chases me around the room.

When my father comes; it hides.

Grandpa's Farm in Iowa

I'm going to Grandpa's farm in Iowa.

Wandering up and down the aisles on the train in January 1958, the California Zephyr. People asked me and I told them—

"I'm going to Grandpa's farm in Iowa."

From Emeryville, California to Ottumwa, Iowa. Snow on the Rockies; deep ravines; a scary dark tunnel. But I mostly remembered—

"I'm going to Grandpa's farm in Iowa."

Why did people always lean forward in their seats to ask— 'where ya going?'—and smile when I tell them? I think. And why did I smile in thinking about it?

Maybe I smiled because of the cats on the farm. In the city, cats were forbiden—maybe because cats got to have birds and mice and wild stuff to eat . . .

Maybe I smiled because of the mulberry trees on the farm. In the city, mulberry trees are hard to find. I don't think city folks even know about mulberries—they seem more like blueberry people.

Maybe I smiled because back on the farm we had Grandma's chicken and noodles, and a box of freshly baked chocolate chip cookies in the fridge. In the city, my mother fixed some great macaroni and cheese, but store-bought cookies taste dry and crunchy while fresh-baked cookies stay soft and moist. The farm was like having root beer and watermelon every day.

I smile thinking about hand pumps to pump, snow drifts to jump in, relatives to visit, and church services to dress up for. Where else do you learn about Daniel in the lion's den and Jonah in the whale? Every day was an adventure on the farm.

But the big reason I smile is because on the farm everyone knew my name, listened to my stories, and helped me feel at home.

"I'm going to Grandpa's farm in Iowa."

Albany, California

*A*t age four in 1958 in Albany, California, I had a bright red wagon like most boys and dreamed of riding my wagon down the hill outside our apartment. My mother told me not to ride it down the hill.

"You are a scaredy-cat. I double dare you," my two-year old sister, Diane, told me.

Tired of pushing and pulling that wagon, I wanted to ride it so one day I got in and rode it down the hill steering with the handle. Faster and faster I went until I reached the corner where I turned the handle to the right to follow the sidewalk, but the wagon turned over, threw me out, and my knees were scraped but good. I cried and cried as I pulled my wagon up the hill to our apartment with one hand on my knee. And my mother came running and bandaged me up.

Our apartment bathroom had a stand-alone, white ceramic tub in which I loved to run the water and race my battery-powered speedboat.

"Let me play," my sister asked.

Why do girls always want to do boy stuff? I think. *I hated to share my boat because the batteries ran down quickly and my parents always told me that I had to wait until Christmas to get new ones. So I told her—*

"*It really feels good to put soap in your eyes.*"

She tried and she cried.

Then, my mother came running.

Oakland, California

*D*ad brought home amazing things.

After we moved to married student housing Oakland, California in 1959 when I was five, my father bought a turntable and subscribed to a mail-order collection of classical music albums, which arrived about once a month. Evenings after putting me to bed, he played his albums and I learned to enjoy classical music. Compositions, such as Wagner's *"Flight of the Valkyries"* and Tchaikovsky's *"1812 Overture,"* kept me awake and later inspired me to study music.

One day my father bought a black and white television that let us watch famous people talk in our living room. People like Billy Graham who said he would wait if we would *"come on down."* Or President Eisenhower, the retired general who came on now and then to tell us about things going on here and there. But I found kid shows like *"Romper Room,"* the *"Micky Mouse Club,"* and *"Captain Kangaroo"* more interesting.

My father collected interesting rocks, sea shells, stamps, and coins, and so did I. The teenage boys who lived in the apartment upstairs collected butterflies, insects, and model ships, cars, and airplanes that they built themselves and I loved to hang out with them. When the boys moved away, I missed hearing about their hobbies and got upset. Whenever I made friends, they moved away.

"How come I don't have a brother to play with?" I asked my parents repeatedly.

My mother and father tried to help me find my own hobbies. My mother bought me a butterfly net which I used to catch bugs and stuff, like the green parakeet that landed in the grass outside the recreation building across the street. My father helped me build balsa-wood, airplanes models that I could build and fly, but loneliness seemed to be my only friend.

The Seat

Kindergarten in Oakland in 1959 unsettled me.

To get to class I walked east down the street out of the neighborhood, across a busy road past lots of palm trees, then left around the corner, and up to the building. I then walked around to the other side of the building, up the steps, and into my classroom, where my chair was located in the middle of the room. I proudly walked to school myself after the first week.

But I missed my friend, Sarah, who lived in our apartment building and attended a school closer to home, north of the neighborhood and up the hill. One day Sarah told me that their classroom had an extra seat and invited me to go to school with her, which I happily did.

As we walked up the hill, a man in a car offered us a ride. As Sarah seemed ready to accept this invitation, I told the man— *"no thanks"*—like my mother told me and kept walking. I often wondered what might have happened had I not been there.

Once we arrived at school, we walked around the side of the building, up the steps, and into the room. I found the empty seat against the wall and sat in it.

As I looked around the classroom, I recognized many

students from the neighborhood. Sarah enjoyed having me in class and she asked why I attended the other school. I told her: *"I registered too late."*

The teacher noticed me and kept asking me questions—

"What's your name? Where do you live? What school do you go to?"

None of these questions made sense because the class had an empty seat and I found it first.

Pretty soon my mother came and drove me back to the other school, where my teacher met us.

"You missed the Christmas party," my teacher told me.

"How could it be Christmas without any snow."

"It does not snow in California."

She might have told me that Jesus' birthday comes with or without snow and I might have understood.

"Did you save me some goodies?"

There were no goodies and I missed being in Sarah's class.

Christmas in Iowa

I loved to stand in the back seat of my father's lime green 1953 Chrysler and look over his shoulder as he drove.

I saw everything!

As a I stood there, I imagined driving my own car—not a bicycle or a Vesta or a pickup but a great big powerful car, with a shiny hood ornament, white-walled tires, and plenty of head room for a fedora—just like my father's.

But Fords work better on gravel hills.

Chrysler's don't like hills, like the hill along rural route 2 outside Oskaloosa, Iowa. I saw everything. My father drove up the hill; then, he rolled back down. He drove up the hill; then, he rolled back down again. Then, he parked the car next to the post box to walk up the hill in the snow in December 1959.

"Stephen, wait in the car and take care of your mother and sister." Dad told me after I offered to go along.

While I waited, I thought it odd that a little hill challenged my father's big, powerful Chrysler.

After a bit, my grandfather drove down the hill with his Ford 2N, four-cylinder tractor. My father stood on the swinging draw-bar in the back and he could see everything looking over my grandfather's shoulder. They chained the car to the tractor and towed it up the hill to the farm house in time for dinner.

Mad Dog

*I*n early 1960, I often roamed around the apartment complex and the recreation center in married student housing. Next to the center stood a sand box; behind it was a baseball field; and underneath it lived a guinea pig. I tried several times to catch that guinea pig, thinking that I could lure him out with pieces of bread and trap him in an empty box propped up with a stick attached to a string that I waited to pull.

When I felt adventurous, I crossed the baseball field to play by a creek with soft, black mud, which disappeared into a tunnel under a road. I seldom crossed the road for fear of the dairy cattle chained up and grazing on the grass that grew among the foundations of now demolished apartments.

One day a cow got loose and wandered through the neighborhood. Neighbors and kids ran every which way screaming bloody murder at the sight of this cow roaming loose. The running and screaming went on until my father came home and calmly led the cow back to the field, where it returned to grazing.

I normally stayed clear of the cows, preferring to hang out by the creek, building dams, or skipping rocks on the water. One day, I remember a friend dared me to step into the water; then he dared me to wade deeper and deeper in the water. When

I refused to go further, he ran off.

About a block down from our apartment, I used to climb a short cherry tree with low hanging branches. One afternoon an angry dog chased me through that yard and, terrified, I climbed up that tree to get away. My mother later told me that the same dog bit a friend of mine, Sarah. She had to get painful stomach shots, but before I got to ask her about it we moved away.

Yellow Wax Beans

When I spent summers on the farm in Iowa with my grandparents, we often gardened together. In the vegetable garden, Grandpa Frank planted sweat peas, yellow wax beans, tomatoes, radishes, rhubarb, and pumpkin. Along the side of the house, Grandma Gertrude planted roses, gladiolas, and morning glories. I mostly pulled weeds and talked to my grandparents, as we worked.

Although my father visited the farm only briefly during the summer, his name always came up in our garden conversations. When he studied at Iowa State, my father planted grape vines along the fence in the back of the garden, a row of apple and peach trees off to the left side, and a cherry tree in front.

Garden work normally picked up towards the end of the summer when fruits and vegetables ripened and needed to be harvested. Grandma packed her beans in square, plastic containers to put in the basement freezer and canned the fruit in mason jars to place on a shelf, also in the basement. If she had any extra garden produce, Grandma saved it to trade with her favorite sister, Nettie, who raised sweet corn and kept chickens on her farm near Leighton, which was northwest of Oskaloosa.

Even when we visited on gardening business, Nettie

showed us her china plate collection.

"*Isn't this plate nice? Your father brought this plate to me from Tokyo,*" she would tell me.

This was her way of reminding me that whenever we traveled to an exotic place, she wanted us to bring a souvenir plate for her collection. Similarly, Grandma Gertrude required a silver spoon.

After the china tour, Nettie served us coffee and a piece of one of her special cakes. Then, we changed into work clothes and got down to harvesting sweet corn and dressing chickens.

The day's work proceeded in steps. While the men started a charcoal fire out back and picked bushels of corn, the women heated large pails of boiling water and set up the picnic tables with the necessary utensils.

Preparing the corn required that we shuck the ears to remove the husk and the silk. Then, we cut the corn kernels off the ears with a parry knife.

After I cut myself with the paring knife, Nettie bandaged me up.

"*Stephen, you are pretty good at husking, why don't you focus on that?*"

So I did and gladly.

Dressing chickens took more time and involved a bigger mess. Nettie's husband, Corny, cut off the chickens' heads with a knife and tied the chicken by the feet to the clothes lines outside. The headless chickens flapped their wings for a couple minutes splashing blood everywhere. When they stopped, he put them in large, metal bucket of boiling water for a few minutes to loosen the feathers. Then, we each grabbed a chicken and starting plucking the feathers. Between the wet feathers and the blood, I never took to dressing chickens and much preferred gardening.

As a teenager, I spaded up a garden of my own out back of our house in Maryland, where the red-clay soil made it difficult to grow vegetables other than radishes, pumpkins, and yellow wax beans. Although the radishes and pumpkin never made it to the dinner table, I earned my stripes as a gardener growing yellow wax beans. My little garden never produced enough beans for more than a meal or two; still, yellow wax beans reminded me of summers on the farm and made me feel like a real gardener.

Driving Lesson

One summer afternoon as grandpa and grandma rested after lunch, I slipped out without permission, started up the tractor, and began cultivating a field of soybeans for the first time. After plowing about three rows of beans, the tractor got stuck in a wet spot in the field. Try as I might, the tractor just sank deeper in the mud.

Ashamed of myself having got stuck in the mud, I went to get my grandfather. He tried, but was also unable, to dislodge the tractor from the mud. He then called the neighbor who brought a chain, hooked it to the tractor, and pulled the tractor free with his pickup truck. The job took all afternoon.

In spite of the work I created and inconvenience, neither the neighbor nor my grandfather complained or scolded me, much as I deserved it. While this was first lesson in driving a stick-shift vehicle, what I remember best was grandpa's patience. My sense of forgiveness as a pre-teen was immediate, yet something that I will never forget.

FAMILY ORIGINS

My Name

*I*s a name a blessing, a curse, or prophesy? My first name, Stephen, comes from the Greek word for crown.

The biblical story of Stephen describes him as: *"a man full of faith and of the Holy Spirit"* (Acts 6:5). He was one of the first to serve as a deacon in the church and succeeded in his work *"doing great wonders and signs among the people"* (Acts 6:8). He also persuasively argued for the faith attracting enemies who, unable to debate him, alleged that he planned to destroy the temple in Jerusalem and to change the Law of Moses (Acts 6:10–11). Although never proven or disputed, these charges led to his stoning and martyrdom.

My mother wanted to name me, Wayne, which became my middle name after my grandmother, Gertrude (DeKock) Hiemstra, insisted that I be named, like my father, for her grandfather, Stephanus DeKock, who died the year that I was born.

Stephanus emigrated from the Netherlands (Herwijnen) and settled in Pella, Iowa with his parents in 1856 at the age of seventeen. In August 1862, Stephanus volunteered for the Union Army and served in the Civil War with distinction in the 22rd

Iowa Infantry.

In the DeKock family, the name, Stephen, started with Stephanie, the wife of Philip of Naples in twelfth century France. Her son, Rudolf Chatillon, received the title of Count *LeCocq* from the King of France because Rudolf reported early every day for battle—like a rooster (*le Cocq*). Later (around 1200) Rudolf received a grant of land in Gelderland, Holland and had the title, Le Cocq, translated into the Dutch equivalent, *DeKock*.

As a name, Hiemstra, divides into two parts: *"hiem"* and *"stra"*, which a Frisian friend of mine informed me years ago. *"Hiem"* means home while the *"stra"* indicates a Frisian origin. The Hiemstra family originates in Dokkum, a Frisian city along the North Sea in the Netherlands.

The Frisians have their own, distinctive language which, unlike other local dialects, shares little in common with either German or Dutch. The Frisians kept their independence from surrounding nations until the Dutch revolt against Spain in 1568 during the reformation.

My grandfather, Frank Henry Hiemstra, spoke Frisian along with Dutch but he insisted that his sons speak only English, like other Americans. To separate the family from daily, ethnic Dutch influences—a very Frisian idea—Frank moved the family down the road from Pella to a farm near Oskaloosa, Iowa. The family began attending Central Reformed Church in downtown Oskaloosa, which began holding services in English in 1953, the year of my birth.

Kaffietijd

*M*ore than a snack, coffee time structured our lives and became an institution where my fondest memories of family life unfolded and I got a glimpse of heaven.

On weekdays, at nine in morning, at three in the afternoon, and around eight in the evening, my grandmother, Gertrude Hiemstra, prepared coffee for the adults, cocoa for the kids, and goodies for everyone. The goodies included homemade lemon bars, chocolate chip cookies, or strawberry short cake topped with ice cream. Choice, we always got a choice.

Whether knitting, feeding the calves, or pulling weeds in the garden, everyone paused, came in the house, got cleaned up, and talked. No one was excluded; everyone was invited; and conversation was required, even if briefly, six times a day.

On Sundays, coffee time got more involved. No one dared to skip Sunday school or leave town before lunch at grandma's house. So we attended church at nine-fifteen, but took a break for snacks during Sunday school. After church, we normally changed from our Sunday best into more comfortable clothes before lunch. After changing one thing led to another and by the time the adults called us for lunch, we kids might be hiding in the attic or chasing each other around the yard. When we refused to come for lunch, the adults bribed us to come with reminders of coffee time after lunch.

Sometimes Sunday coffee times were delayed until after the cuckoo clock chimed at four o'clock. A late coffee time almost always involved better snacks and required fold up trays and breaking out the card tables, which would be used later for playing hearts or board games. On occasion, the piano was played and ice cream churned by hand. When we complained about helping churn, the adults would tease us.

"Kids today are so spoiled by that store-bought ice cream," they reminded us.

Sunday coffee time became more formal when we celebrated the birthdays of my grandparents and their many siblings. Because grandma and grandpa each had eight siblings who lived around Pella, Iowa, a Dutch colony settled in 1847. The siblings pooled birthday celebrations several times a year and collectively made the twenty mile trip to Oskaloosa. When the *"Pella crowd"* visited, a leisurely three or four hour visit followed where no one hurried and everyone naturally wore their Sunday best. Formalities took distinctive phases, which moved from greetings, to eating, to discussions and board games, and then to goodbyes.

After the formal greetings, the women gathered in the

kitchen to properly set out their signature dishes, such as my grandmother's steaming hot, chicken and noodles. Meanwhile, the men sat in the living room talking about the latest news or the market prices for corn, soybeans, hogs, or cattle. The kids ran this way or that, but often we retreated to the basement to horse around without soiling our clothes.

The eating phase always started with a blessing for the food. When my uncle, Pastor John, visited, we were treated to a few introductions and announcements (or a scripture reading) followed by a pastoral prayer. Otherwise, my grandfather, Frank, simply gave thanks.

Having blessed the food, we grabbed a plate and the family crowd snaked in line around the kitchen helping ourselves to the sandwiches, casseroles, apple sauce, and potato salad. Grandma normally served a lime or strawberry punch—iced in a crystal bowl, ladled with a crystal dipper, and enjoyed in a crystal cup. Then, the adults assembled in the living room seated behind folding trays with their plates and cups carefully balanced. Meanwhile, the kids sat around the kitchen table and ate together unsupervised. The women later served coffee with the dessert.

The end of dessert marked the beginning of pointed discussions. Great Uncle John, the local county commissioner, frequently chided me about the cushy government job that I might in Washington D.C. get after graduation. Of course, I had other ideas. At one point in my sophomore year, for example, I announced my intention to study comparative literature, instead of agricultural economics like my father.

A couple of embarrassing seconds of silence passed.

"Comparative literature? What's that?" Great Aunt Nelly inquired.

Nelly usually voiced what others only thought. Over the coming year, her question helped motivate me to find a new major.

Some discussions took a less serious turn.

"Have year heard about that new government program that they cooked up in Washington?" someone asked.

"No. What program are we talking about?"

"In the future, social security checks will be issued along with a prescription for birth control pills."

". . . ah-huh."

Everyone took part in discussions and often board games marked an informal end to our gatherings. Those less interested in playing hearts, domino's, or board games headed for the door, as regular as Grandfather's daily bowl of *All Bran* cereal soaked in chocolate milk. Goodbyes then proceeded and, weather permitting, farewells included walking the most distant travelers out to their cars.

As the years went by, coffee time died out.

My parents struggled to imitate coffee time when my grandparents visited, but practice makes perfect and neglect leaves one neglectful. Interruptions during attempts at coffee time made conversation difficult; activities likewise cut into the leisure time. On the farm, Christmas would last for two weeks, while, in the city, Christmas often dwindled to a meal and an afternoon discussion. We aspired to being relaxed and hospitable, but strived ever more diligently to keep our jobs, pay our bills, and advance our careers in the face of ever-easier, downward mobility. As my grandparents aged, travel distances seemed longer, schedules got more involved, and visits became rare.

Coffee time lived on during visits to Iowa. When my grandfather turned ninety, he had a fender-bender and lost his driver's license. So when I visited, Frank often requested that I drive him from Oskaloosa to Pella to visit Nelly, his younger sister, the family historian, and a live wire. A quick call and Nelly would invite the surviving Pella crowd over to her place for coffee. Thirty minutes later on our arrival, out came the folding trays, the home-made snacks, and the coffee.

Born in 1898, Frank journeyed through three centuries during his 102 years. With his passing, Oskaloosa dropped off my itinerary. Since then, travel has become infrequent and the memory of coffee time became elusive.

Coffee time lives on in the Hiemstra family picnic the first Saturday of August each year in Pella's West Market Park, over the past eighty-six years. Picnic tables shaded under the shelter are cool and I cherish seeing distant relatives. The coffee and the snacks remain the same, but the folding trays, the leisure time, and my grandparents no longer make an appearance.

More than a snack, coffee time (or Kaffietijd as the old folks used to say) built a palace in time that echoes in the memory of my youth.

The Other Stephen Hiemstra

*M*y father, whom I sometimes introduce as the other Stephen Hiemstra, was born on April 17, 1931 during the Great Depression. He grew up on a small, feed-livestock farm in southern Iowa and attended college under the GI Bill.

His education followed a series of apparently serendipitous decisions, which allowed the family to prosper during the move from rural to urban employment. My father was one of the first in his extended family to attend college and he made sure that each of his children also attended. A total of four of us completed doctoral studies: my father, my uncle, my brother, and yours truly.

My father worked for the federal government during a formative period, beginning in the late Eisenhower Administration through the early Reagan Administration, when belief in the positive contribution that government could make reached an historical peak. He strenuously pursued his work writing numerous studies and actively participated in many professional societies.

Because I followed my father into agricultural economics, early in my career I worked hard to distinguish myself from my father.

During my year abroad studying in Germany during graduate school, I felt that I had finally escaped the shadow of my father, but I was wrong. One evening, I attended a doctoral celebration party and as I socialized with my date the department chair walked up to me and invited me to dinner. He had been a classmate of my father at the University of California at Berkeley. At another point, I helped a couple of random American tourists order dinner in a restaurant in Wolfburg, Germany only to find out that the husband was an agricultural economist from Oregon State University and a friend of my father.

Another time a colleague stopped by my office with a journal article dated from 1963 in his hand.

"Steve, did you write this article?"

"Sure. Didn't you know that I am a child prodigy agricultural economist?" I joked.

The article was, of course, one of my father's publications.

After the need to distinguish my career from my father's subsided, it was easier to appreciate the broad scope of his contribution to agricultural economics, particularly in food consumption, demand, and distribution studies.

My father retired from federal service and joined the faculty of what is now the School of Hospitality and Tourism Management at Purdue University as associate professor on August 17, 1983. He taught classes, such as marketing and strategic management, undertook research, and consulted for numerous institutes and firms in the hotel and restaurant industries. He also organized lengthy study trips to Liberia and Hong Kong.

Dad was best known for starting the first doctoral program in the field of hospitality and tourism management anywhere at Purdue University in 1989. His first three students are now faculty members and the program now has 30 doctoral students and leads the field.

The role of my father's Christian faith in his life experience has always been important. The church has traditionally taught personal disciple, commitment in marriage, and generosity in giving, which are all evident in my father's life. My father was a good role model to the rest of us who benefited from his faith and devotion to Christ. He also served a number of churches as elder and in other roles.

More than his church work, however, my father—introduced once as the *"father of USDA's Women, Infants, and Children feeding program"*—embraced the belief that God is the creator of all creation and all knowledge is God's knowledge. For him, economics was more than a career; it was a calling.

A Bit of Irish

My mother, Hazel Fern Hiemstra, grew in Guelph, Ontario Canada, the daughter of Richard Henry and Marietta Salter Deacon. Family history suggests that the Deacons originated in Kilkenny County in southern Ireland, while the name, Deacon, suggests a Scotch-Irish background more typically associated with Northern Ireland.

My mother describes my grandmother as a social butterfly and a devout Baptist who led her to get involved with mission work at a young age. After Marietta died from stomach cancer in 1941 and laid to rest in Wingham, Ontario, my mother began taking care of her younger siblings, although still a teenager herself. My mother later worked in a mission in Washington D.C., continuing her mother's work and setting an example for me. My own mission work with Hispanic day workers remains a tribute to my mother and Marietta.

My oldest connection to the Deacon family was Richard Henry Deacon, who I knew as Grandpa Deacon. Born in 1895, Richard Henry shipped out to Europe in the First World War, but thankfully arrived too late to see combat. After the war, he traveled to work in the Canadian west, but later returned to Guelph, Ontario where he managed the boiler at the University of Guelph. In spite of his lack of education, he loved to read a good *"murder book"* and rescued other books from the boiler fires later reading.

In character and appearance, Grandpa Deacon reminded me of author Mark Twain, who also loved to tell stores. He once visited a graveyard, read a tombstone, and announced that two men had been buried in the same grave because the tombstone read: HERE LIES A LAWYER AND AN HONEST MAN.

Another time, an aluminum siding salesman called the house and Grandpa started up a favorite rant.

"If people would stop wasting their money on such things, then we could buy our country back from the yanks."

After my grandfather told me that story, I asked grandpa where the term, *"canuck"*, came from and he told me the story of Johnny Canuck, a mythical Canadian lumberjack much like the American myth of Paul Bunyan.

My grandfather loved beer and smoked two packs of cigarettes a day until his doctor told him that his emphysema would kill him if he didn't give up the cigarettes. That day he quit smoking and he never smoked again. Still, the rest of his life he wheezed constantly and walked with a limp, having fallen off a ladder behind the house repairing the garage roof.

A true handyman, my grandfather always came to visit and help us when my father had a big home-improvement project, like finishing off a basement. He used to say that *"if you don't have a tool; make one."*

I remember in grade school, for example, that he built me a working cross-bow using only the scraps of wood and metal that we had lying around the house. At that point in my life, I under-appreciated his wisdom and talent. However, later in my career when handed undoable projects and only *"scraps"* to work with, I followed his example and built my own tools. Like Grandpa, I learned to work with the tools at hand.

I always enjoyed visiting Grandpa Deacon because he shared my youthful passion for fishing. When I visited, he early on took me fishing and later on, knowing my fascination with farming, took me to visit in-laws who lived in the country. On one such visit, I remember walking in on relatives as they sat down to lunch that featured soup bones—the meal also included ample supplies of potatoes and turnips, but the bones caught the attention of my youthful eyes. Since then I have never forgotten the hardship posed by poverty.

My grandfather died on February 1, 1980 following complications due to a prostate operation. At his funeral, when they lowered Richard Henry into the grave in Woodlawn Memorial Park in Guelph, I witnessed my mother cry for the first time. Later that evening, my aunt, Judy, took me aside and gave me my grandfather's gold regimental ring. Even as a young man, my fingers were too large to wear the ring and I kept it in a jewelry box, where my wife, Maryam, found it and asked to wear it, as she does to this day.

How soon we forget. Having a bit of Irish in me once meant little more than green beer on Saint Patrick's Day. My exposure to Saint Patrick in seminary fueled an interest in my own Irish roots. Much like Saint Patrick introduced the Irish to Christ in the fifth century and later sparked a revival movement in Europe, I experienced a personal revival. As I did, I realized that I inherited more than just a full head of hair from the Deacon family.

Diane Sue

*A*s the oldest child in the family and the oldest cousin among grandchildren, I grew up surrounded by adults, who gave me a lot of attention at a time when children were to be seen and not heard. Because my father attended graduate school until I entered the first grade and we frequently moved around, it remained hard to make friends my own age. In this 1950s environment, my sister, Diane Sue, was my closest friend.

Diane and I played hide and seek, learned to eat ice cream from cones, and celebrated each other's birthdays together. I will never forget Diane's expression on viewing a pink rabbit cake that my mother baked for her second birthday. Still, close relationships between boys and girls at that time was a bit counter-cultural, at least in the world we lived in.

Diane and I were both baptized in Central Reformed Church in Oskaloosa, Iowa where my dad grew up and my parents were married. During Sunday school classes, boys sat on one side of the room and girls sat on the other, which I remember because in visiting one Sunday I made the mistake of sitting on the girls' side before most people had come in. As the kids filed in, the girls thought it was funny and the boys ridiculed me.

I never repeated that mistake.

Although I always asked to visit the farm during summer vacations and spent most summers until high school there, Diane showed little interest. Perhaps, she did not enjoy going to livestock auctions, gardening, and learning to knit. It's hard to say because we were never nosey about each other's business.

During the school year when we got older, Diane and I took piano lessons together. We also sometimes watched television or played board games together at home and attended youth events and choir together at church. Still, Diane preferred doing girl things, like playing with dolls, while I did boy things, like collecting coins, stamps, and bugs, and playing with the neighbor kids. I became a Cub Scout; she joined the Brownies.

Boys and girls played differently, maintained a different circle of friends, and this was normal, accepted behavior. This pattern was so pronounced that in elementary school the boys had to be forced to dance with girls in gym class. So Diane and I drifted apart after I was about eight years old, although we always maintained an unspoken but close relationship.

John David

$\mathcal{M}$y brother, John David, arrived on April 9, 1963. He was an angel from an early age and the brother that I always wanted even though, he was, ironically, too young to share my childhood blues. Although he was ten years younger than me, I knew him reasonably well even as a tot because we shared the room in the basement in the house on Trexler Road.

In fifth grade a kid down the street sold me half a dozen cherry bombs. I eagerly tested one in the backyard by lighting and placing it in a coffee jar next to my bedroom window, forgetting how powerful such explosives were. The blast knocked me down, bloodied my right side with glass shrapnel, and blew out my bedroom window. The room was also sprayed with glass. John was not there but I remember seeing his crib and feeling guilty about what might have happened had he been there.

Another occasion for guilt came in the middle of the night in the dark, when John got up at one point from bed and began sleep walking around the room. I freaked out, began screaming, and mom ran downstairs and turned on the light. Poor John woke unaware of what had happened and began crying. Mom comforted us both and we all went back to bed.

Another guilt-laden incident happened when John was a youngster and I was in high school. John climbed up the steps in a tree behind the house where I had attempted to build a tree-house years earlier. The step collapsed; John slipped; and an exposed nail sliced the skin in John's leg open from the ankle to the knee.

By the time I heard about it, John was sitting the kitchen. My mother held onto him as I cleaned and bandaged up his leg, holding the skin together and taping it together inch by inch. I was surprised that there was not more blood, but John did not cry. The emergency room doctor that treated John later complimented my work and praised my Scout training.

When I was young, I was allowed to play baseball but mom told me that football was too violent. Notwithstanding, John went on to play football for the New Carrollton Boy's Club at the age of seven. By high school John became a star athlete, quarterbacking the only winning team in twenty years, and president of his class for several years running. Instead of being my younger brother, I became known around town as his older brother, which was fine with me. I always wanted a brother.

My Lovely Wife

*M*y wife, Maryam, was the youngest of nine siblings and grew up in Iran near Ahvaz where her father, Farajollah Hajatpour, worked as a chemical engineer for British Petroleum. Her mother, Naranji Karemi, cared for the children and came from the politically important, Bahktiari tribe, which has its own dialect of Farsi, remained nomadic even in modern times, and stubbornly clung to its Zoroastrian religion until the 1600s. When her father retired from the oil refinery, the family moved to Tehran after her oldest brother, Faramarz, received a promotion.

Families in Iran are close because life can be challenging. Her father was orphaned at the age of eleven. Although he came from a good family, his only brother had passed away and the relatives that cared for him cheated him out of most of his inheritance. Still, he worked hard, earned an education for himself, and used his earnings to educate his kids and to invest in farmland, because he loved horses. Her father also loved to take long evening walks commenting on the upkeep of houses and businesses that he passed, something Maryam still does.

Maryam's mother also had her share of challenges, having raised nine children and lost three others in infancy. She grew up with three other siblings, but her mother had given birth to sixteen. Life expectancy in Iran has historically been short by American standards and Maryam only knew one of grandparents, a grandmother who died when Maryam was in high school.

Maryam had several near-death experiences herself as a child. At the age of four, she sustained severe burns to her face in a cooking fire. At six, she witnessed the drowning of a friend and got extremely sick with malaria. The closest she came to death, however, came at age five.

Ahvaz has a climate like Texas and the homes are surrounded with marble stone walls. To cope with the heat, people customarily slept outdoors at night in the summertime. One night a black scorpion the size of a small crab climbed up on Maryam's bed and stung her three times. Her brother rushed her immediately to the hospital where she received twenty-six injections of anti-venom. Even still, her fingers curled up in a fist as the paralysis effects of the venom went through her body. Several neighborhood children known to the family died from similar attacks. She survived, but to this day remains afraid of large insects and other creeping critters.

As the youngest in the family, Maryam was always daddy's little girl and her older siblings also spoiled her. As a dedicated student in school, she remained the teacher's helper, which in Iran meant that she took responsibility for cleaning the chalkboards and taking roll. As a high school graduate preparing to study abroad, Maryam once visited a psychic in Tehran who predicted that Maryam would one-day marry an American.

After leaving Iran, Maryam studied for a year at Halton College in the United Kingdom and another year at United States International University in Los Angeles, which has a large community of Iranians. When expenses started to become a problem, she transferred to Detroit Institute of Technology (DIT) where she lived with her brother, Ghasem, and sister, Azar.

Maryam last visited Iran in 1978. Three days after she returned to Detroit on September 3, the Shah imposed martial law in Tehran. In the turbulent months that followed, her father was hospitalized in Tehran with a twisted intestine. This condition, called volvulus, results in a bowel obstruction causing abdominal pain, bloating, vomiting, constipation, and bloody stool, and requires emergency surgery. Between power outages and doctor strikes, her father did not receive the care he needed and died a painful death.

For a number of months the family sheltered Maryam and her siblings from news of his death. Eventually, Maryam called around the family to find him and discovered a pattern of deception. Confronted with her discovery, the family acknowledged that her father had died.

Maryam grieved her father's death in absentia, both because Islamic Law requires immediate internment and because political chaos made travel nearly impossible.

The Iranian Revolution posed a financial hardship for Maryam and her siblings related to the international embargo imposed on Iran after the Iranian hostage crisis (November 4, 1979, to January 20, 1981). Family financial support continued through a distant relative in Saudi Arabia who arranged financial transfers, subject to a fee of close to fifty percent. Financial hardship in Iran eventually forced Maryam, her brother and sister to delay their studies and seek work. Still, Maryam graduated with a bachelor's degree in chemistry from DIT in 1982 and a second bachelor's degree in chemical engineering from Wayne State University in 1983.

ELEMENTARY SCHOOL

King Street

*I*n 1960 we moved to Alexandria, Virginia where we rented a townhouse on King Street and I started first grade at the age of six. My class had two other boys named Stephen so the teacher decided to call us—Stephen, Steve, and Stevie. The teacher also required us to take morning naps on throw rugs, like a bunch of tots. Needless to say, I did not enjoy my introduction to first grade.

In the fall President Kennedy won the election and later on Inauguration Day we received three feet of snow. I spent the day making snowmen and jumping into waist-high snow drifts while my father and mother watched the speeches and parades on television. Once my hands got too cold to play in the snow, I joined my parents in watching the inauguration.

In the spring, my father bought me a bicycle. The sidewalks in our subdivision weaved in and around the townhouses so the first time that I peddled my bike down a sidewalk, I peddled too fast, failed to negotiate a corner, and slammed into a brick wall. Stubborn, I got up and kept trying until I could bike anywhere that I wanted.

Late in the spring we had a science fair and I constructed

an exhibit using the best butterflies in my collection. After my presentations were over, I went home. When I returned to school the next day, I found that many of my butterflies had been broken into pieces. Worse, I did not place well in the competition. Upset, several years passed before I participated in another science fair.

Late in the year, someone suggested that I needed a girlfriend so one morning I walked around the cafeteria table looking to find one.

"Will you be my girlfriend?" I asked one girl.

"No."

"Will you be my girlfriend?" I asked another.

"No."

. . . Finally, a girl agreed. After that we played together in school and out until that summer, when my family moved to Maryland.

Prince George's Post

*M*y sister, Karen arrived on July 7, 1961. Soon thereafter, we moved into a three-bedroom house in the *Kings Woods* subdivision on Trexler Road, which backed up to Greenbelt Park in Lanham, Maryland. As the second family to move into the neighborhood, we lived next to the model homes and got to watch the split-level ramblers being built further down the street.

About a year later, someone asked if I wanted to carry papers for the Prince George's Post. The opportunity to earn spending money appealed to me and I immediately agreed. Although I knew nothing about delivering newspapers, I knew a lot about the neighborhood. As one of the first kids on the block, I met all the new neighbors and their kids as they moved in.

The Post came out on Thursdays and cost a nickel. Once a month I collected twenty cents and earned a nickel. With one hundred and twenty customers, I earned about six dollars a month.

Once I saved enough money, I bought a canvas carrying bag with a shoulder strap. The papers came tied up in a bundle weighing probably forty pounds, which was too heavy to carry by hand. With my bag, I could ride my bike and carry the entire bundle in one trip.

Later, I used my earnings to buy model airplanes and collect old coins, hobbies too expensive to undertake on my allowance alone. At my father's suggestion, I opened a saving account at the bank and deposited money left over at the end of the month.

Most of my customers lived on Trexler and Nashville Roads, but a few lived on Wilhelm Drive and Jodie Street. I tried drumming up new subscribers on other streets by leaving a few sample papers each week at different houses, but it never seemed to work out.

Like the Apostle Paul who traveled about making and selling tents in the marketplace in each city he visited (Acts 18:1–4), I got to know many people through my newspaper business. My newspaper business taught me how business gets done, how to talk with people, and the value of customer loyalty. I delivered the Post from 1961 until 1968.

Cowboys and Indians

*I*n elementary school, I played outdoor games a lot in the street and neighborhood, where it took a lot of pounding on doors to gather enough neighbor kids to play. Oftentimes, it was hard to get kids to give up watching television long enough to play Red Rover, cowboys and Indians, or baseball.

Red Rover began with picking teams and, once picked, the teams stood about 30 feet apart and took turns chanting: *"Red Rover, Red Rover, please send Charlie over!"* Then, the chanting team lined up and locked hands; then, Charlie who had been called out from the other team, ran full speed at the opposing line and tried to crash through their hands. If Charlie broke through the line, he returned to his team taking a captive team member with him. If not, he joined the chanting team. Then, the other team took a turn chanting. The game ended when one team acquired all the players. Red Rover could get embarrassing, if your friends picked everyone else or you were the last to get called.

I preferred baseball, which focused less on picking and more on playing. In school-yard games, I hit well and had a strong throwing arm, but I started little league at eleven. By then, many of the boys had already played in leagues for several years and my natural talent proved no longer competitive.

Playing cowboys and Indians required little more than a cap gun, a bow, and a few arrows. Most of the time, we chased each other around making a lot of noise until everyone got tired. Other times it was fun just dressing up like a cowboy.

One afternoon, my mother let me wear my cowboy hat, holster, and cap-gun on a trip to the K-Mart in New Carrollton.

"*Say, that is a mighty fine six-shooter you have there. Do you mind if I take a look?*" The policeman said as we entered the store.

"*Sure,*" I said, handing him the gun.

He took the gun, looked it over as if he had been handed a priceless collector's item, and handed it back to me.

"*You take care,*" he said as we walked on.

One of my favorite television shows was the *Lone Ranger.* I read every book in the series that I could find in local stores and never missed the show.

In my favorite episode, a gang of outlaws ambushed the Texas Rangers, shot them all, and left those wounded to die in the hot Texas sun. Tonto heard the noise, watched what happened a safe distance, and investigated the scene when the fight ended. Like the Good Samaritan, he rescued the survivor—the Lone Ranger—whom he brought home and nursed back to health, much to his tribe's dismay. The Lone Ranger and Tonto then became good friends and traveled together finding adventure everywhere they went. I always wished that I had a friend like that.

My Friend, Charlie

*I*n the second grade at Wildercroft Elementary School in Riverdale, Maryland, Mrs. S. learned that I enjoyed standing in front of the class too much for it to serve as a disciplinary strategy. So she returned to having me stand with my face in a corner or whacked me with a ruler on open hands, if I shot rubber bands or talked too much.

Still, I enjoyed school.

At one point the whole school assembled outside on the playground to watch Astronaut John Glenn fly overhead in spite of the February weather. His space capsule soared across the sky like a daytime Venus—bright, conspicuous, and full of hope. Space travel thrilled me and I wanted to become an astronaut.

In second grade I met Charlie, who became my first close friend outside the family. He lived on a farm far enough down Good Luck Road to seem like a rural outpost, but close enough that my mother could drop me off afternoons or weekends.

The farm consisted of an old farmhouse, a garage, a shed, and a lot of untended fields. His family didn't keep livestock, chickens, or machinery, but the gravel road out front reminded me of Iowa, where I felt most at home. Charlie and I wandered those fields talking, looking for adventure, and shooting his BB gun.

Charlie was an only child and a lonely kid. Like me, he was unfamiliar with the language of emotion and telling stories, even familiar Biblical stories. We had no quick cure for loneliness, but for a season we were friends.

During our explorations, we discovered an abandoned, plywood tree house down the road that looked as if someone had lived there. Scattered around the place were flares that we confused with dynamite so we left in a hurry.

"You are different from the other boys who run wild and shoot BBs every which way in the air." Charlie told me.

"Really? What kind of idiot wastes good BBs?"

Normally, I bought and paid for BBs myself, but I also had developed a certain respect for guns that went beyond saving money.

During a prior summer in Iowa, I shot a pigeon sitting in the rafters of my grandfather's barn with my BB gun. It fluttered to the ground confused; I caught the bird and put it in a cage. I realized later that I had shot out its left eye, which the bird hid from me by always turning to look at me with the right eye. When I realized what I had done, I was ashamed. After that, while I still enjoyed shooting and hunting, I began to consider a gun a lethal weapon.

Charlie's parents appreciated my visits. His mother smiled as she made us lunch while his father quietly sat at the dining room table and worked on papers. Later, when we were in the fourth grade, Charlie's father put a gun to his head and shot himself.

"What happened to your father?" I asked him.

"I don't want to talk about it?"

I never learned why his father killed himself and no one else discussed the matter with me. Charlie remained alone with his grief and I provided him no comfort. Soon, Charlie and his mother moved to Bethesda, which put an end to my farm visits.

I missed Charlie.

After a while, I looked up Charlie's last name in the telephone book and called the different numbers in Bethesda until I found him.

"Charlie?"

"Hey, Steve. How are you doing?"

We talked briefly, but the circumstances of our lives had diverged. The topics that we normally talked about—friends, school activities, and the farm—had been taken from us. After we finished talking, we never spoke again.

Nemesis

*I*n the fall of 1963, I transferred to Margret Brent Elementary School in New Carrollton, Maryland. There I met Brad who shared my interest in science and we each built a working telegraph for class that year. The following year, however, he had a different teacher and we seldom interacted. Worse, he started hanging around with a gang that enjoyed picking fights on the playground during recess.

One day in recess, he threw sand in my face, grabbed the kick ball that I had been playing with, and ran off. I cleaned the sand out of my eyes and went back to retrieve my ball, and we started fighting. Brad began throwing punches while his gang tried to slow me down by jumping on my back. I threw one after another of them off my back and punched Brad. We hit each other until we were both drenched in blood and the teachers broke up the fight.

The teachers sent us to the aid station where the nurse cleaned us up. Brad fought with his eyes shut while I watched what was happening so it was all his blood. After cleaning us up, they sent us to the principal who called our parents and sent us home.

Brad never reformed after grade school, but he kept a

nervous eye on me as he picked on other guys. In eighth grade, we shared a shop class together, where he spent his time sharpening wooden knives on the sander and threatening other students. The teacher never intervened to stop him. In high school, I remember seeing him a couple times, but he soon disappeared into the juvenile detention system. I never saw him again.

Salvation on Trexler Road

Our house on Trexler Road backed up to Greenbelt National Park where I lived in a basement room. From the comfort of my bed at night, I could look out and see the tree line against the stars.

During the day, neighborhood kids ran in gangs through these woods armed with homemade swords and shields, hiding in forts that they had built for protection. But roofless forts offered little protection against rocks and dirt clods tossed into the air like mortar rounds during summer gang fights that often ended with screams and crying. As kids, we could be vicious and showed little mercy towards those we injured.

In March 1966, my parents took me to a theater in Constitutional Hall downtown in Washington D.C. to preview a movie, *The Cross and the Switchblade,* about gang violence in New York City and a young pastor, David Wilkerson, who cared enough to get involved.

Living out of his car, Wilkerson focused his witness on a gang, the Mau Maus, and one of their leaders, Nicky Cruz. Nicky had a mean streak, expressed lots of attitude, and led the gang into turf fights over territory, like Central Park. When Wilkerson arranged a peace conference among the gangs in a local theater,

Nicky planned with other gang leaders to turn the event into a fight to the death among rival gangs.

When the day came for the conference, the gangs prepared for the fight. Unaware that the theater had been locked, Wilkerson began to preach to the gangs, boys and girls, who pretended to listen. All except Nicky, who listened to the pastor's words and found himself overwhelmed by God's love. When the fight began, he stood between the gangs.

"Did you hear what the pastor just said?" Nicky asked them.

He had clearly accepted Christ into his life and immediately appealed to the gangs to make peace. Not all gang members were happy about it, but the planned fight never happened and many gang members accepted Christ into their lives that day.

In Nicky Cruz's fights and bravado, I could see myself—when he bled, I bled; when he was afraid, I was afraid; when he came to Christ, I came to Christ. Years passed before I understood the importance of my decision to follow Christ, but as my journey of faith progressed, I became increasingly aware of God's presence in my life.

After the film ended, I answered an alter call there in the theater. The following summer, I completed a mail-order Bible study prepared by the Billy Graham Society. In the fall, I joined the communicant's class at Riverdale Presbyterian Church, where my family had begun attending services.

In the class, the pastor taught us the Heidelberg Catechism for about twelve weeks and afterwards the session quizzed us on it. Why I had decided to join the church never came up in discussion. I remember enjoying the opportunity to get to know the pastor, who soon thereafter retired, but remember little of the class or my classmates or any encouragement to practice evangelism.

From the study, one verse resonated over the years:

> For God so loved the world, that he gave his only Son, that whoever believes in him should not perish but have eternal life. (John 3:16)

Salvation had come to Trexler Road.

Music Lessons

*I*n August 1951 my father and mother met during a couples' skate at a roller-skating rink in Guelph, Ontario, Canada where my mother grew up. At the time, she enjoyed singing with an orchestra and playing popular music on the piano.

When we lived on Trexler Road, my father bought an old, second-hand piano, which sat in the recreation room outside my room. In the evening, my mother used to play hymns, like *How Great Thou Art*, and songs, like *One Enchanted Evening* from South Pacific, on that piano. Those tunes became so familiar I still catch myself singing them during quiet moments.

One morning my father backed out of the driveway on Trexler Road and crashed into a car, driven by a neighbor—a Mrs. C, who lived down the street and taught piano. Tail lights shattered and scattered all over the road. Soon thereafter, my sister, Diane, and I began visiting Mrs. C for lessons.

While some people might have taken this accident as an opportunity to launch a lawsuit, my father treated the accident as an inconvenient introduction to a new and helpful neighbor.

"Lord, why have you brought me to this time and this place?" I often pray when my circumstances baffle me or *"acci-*

dents" happen.

For years I dreamed of playing piano and leading people in singing. But, in practicing my lessons I played piano about half an hour a day and fretted about missing this or that television show. The spirit was willing but the flesh was weak (Matt 26:41). In the fifth grade when I took up trombone lessons, I gave up the piano.

Still, important seeds had been sown. My early appreciation and training in music led me to hear God's voice most clearly through music, especially inspirational hymns.

Between Sundays

*A*fter I confessed my faith in Christ and joined Riverdale Presbyterian Church in 1967, I immediately forsook violence and distanced myself from those that practiced it. I also participated more actively in church youth programs, sang in the youth choir, and pledged money to the church, as was expected of young Christian men. But like many others, I struggled to live out my faith and to practice real hospitality and evangelism beyond the boundaries of cultural Christianity.

I knew a boy named Jimmy, who might today be referred to as having special needs. When he heard that I was learning to play piano, he wanted to learn too and one day I volunteered to teach him after school. Knowing that Christians should be compassionate and charitable to people—which I interpreted more narrowly as being really nice—I wanted to help him learn piano.

When Jimmy arrived after school, my mother welcomed him in our home and prepared snacks for us. But when we were alone, she awkwardly asked: *"Is Jimmy one of your friends?"* Jimmy and I went straight to the piano where I taught him a few notes and how to play a C major scale. We spent about half an hour before he left and went home. Thinking about my mother's question, I never invited him back.

By contrast, my mother really liked David, who lived two doors down from us. David was tall, thin, and quiet, and he was always at home. His father was a popular local pastor and a ham radio operator, and his mother was as sweet as the snacks that she offered up.

David and I traded baseball cards, marbles, and stamps, but he was socially awkward. He never seemed interested in playing games with the other kids in the neighborhood and expressed little interest in chess, my favorite game. I spent time with David, but we were not close.

Living out Christian values at home back then primarily meant going to church, saying our prayers, and applying the Ten commandments. As kids, we focused particularly on honoring our fathers and mothers. We also tried to understand other people by *"walking in their shoes,"* but our own social skills and context limited our ability to do much more than project our values on them.

Fifth Grade

In fifth grade I noticed that my outlook on life differed from most other boys, although I had trouble understanding why. It never occurred to me that reading my Bible on a regular basis set me apart.

At the end of the third grade, Grace Presbyterian Church, presented me with a Revised Standard Version Bible. In this Bible, I underlined passages that I felt were important. As I grew older, I stopped underlining in books because my teachers taught respect for school-issued textbooks, but my Bible records my earlier underlyings. As a young person, I particularly liked the Book of Proverbs.

My seriousness as a young person showed up in the Cub Scouts, where I earned my Wolf, Bear, Lion, and Weblos badges. Participating in Weblos, short for *"We'll Be Loyal Scouts,"* distinguished me from other Cub Scouts because many skipped Weblos to join Boy Scouts at age eleven. Most Scouts spent their time playing with their friends, running wild during meetings, and earned few badges.

I also took music seriously. When my principle announced that a glee club had been formed, I volunteered immediately because I loved to sing while I worked and I associated music with God's presence. At first, the club remained small, but when students noticed that club members got out of class, everyone wanted to join and rehearsals became chaotic, taking the fun out of learning music. Frustrated with the constant disruptions during rehearsal, I quit the glee club and returned to class where I sat quietly with the teacher and finished my homework.

Although I gave up the glee club, I started playing the trombone and joined the school band. I also began singing in the youth choir at Riverdale Presbyterian Church (RPC) and later took voice lessons with the choir director. From that point forward, I spent most Sunday and Wednesday evenings in activities at church.

On other evenings, I watched action television shows, like *The Gallant Men, The Untouchables,* and *The Man from U.N.C.L.E.,* one of many spy shows popular with boys at the time.

At school some of the guys started hanging out and being secretive. When I inquired why, they invited me into their secret society, which looked out for foreign spies and carried water-pistols filled with salt-water in case of attack. Another serious young man, Jonathan L. Jenkins, who attended RPC and shared my interest in music, master-minded this secret society. As time passed, we became best friends and I just called him Jon.

PART 2: NEVER ALONE

JUNIOR AND SENIOR HIGH SCHOOL

Shaken and Stirred

Charles Carroll Junior High School in New Carrollton, Maryland was larger and had more students than the elementary schools feeding it. Seventh grade differed from grade school because, instead of having a single teacher, a classroom, and a desk, we had six teachers in six classrooms, and a locker. Organized like a factory assembly-line, when the bell rang, we moved efficiently from class to class storing extra books, notes, and personal items in our lockers along the way.

School also started with a bell. Before the bell, we lined up outside the doors and waited. At one point, some friends and I snuck in early to drop off and pick up things in our locker but the vice principal (VP) caught us. He slammed one of our lockers shut and we took off running. No one wanted to be caught by the VP, who was responsible for school discipline and took his job seriously.

The VP spent the day wandering the halls, catching rule breakers, and reminding them of the rules with the paddle that hung on his wall.

If the VP paddled someone, questions focused not on the punishment, but on the infraction.

"What did you do wrong?" People typically asked.

The dictum—*"spare the rod; spoil the child"*—was well-known and frequently cited *(Prov 13:24)*. The discipline in my junior high school differed little from that Saint Augustine described in his *Confessions* fifteen hundred years ago, who was corporally disciplined repeatedly as a young man for inattention to his studies.

I learned to keep the rules, not from the VP, but from Mr. B., who was popular with students because he wore a stylish crew cut and told great stories in his civic class. But, Mr. B also had a short temper.

One day while Mr. B was writing on the board I shot a spit ball at a classmate and it landed at Mr. B's feet. When Mr. B saw the spit ball, he went nuts. He turned around, grabbed the student in front of me, picked him up by the shoulders, and shook him like a rag doll in front of the class. I am not sure that the student knew why Mr. B got mad at him because he never confronted me about the spit ball, the discipline, or my role in it. For the rest of the period, Mr. B left us to do our homework and no one said a word.

After the incident in Mr. B's class, I lost interest in spit balls and mostly kept the rules. Still, how could I wander through life not reflecting on the rewards and punishments being offered up? Like every other kid, I loathed being subjected to such punishments even when I deserved them and admired those who dished them out.

After I entered college in 1972, the courts ordered school busing to achieve racial integration in Prince George's County, Maryland, where I had attended school. The old standard of discipline disappeared, never to return, in spite of its biblical warrant.

Personal Fitness Merit Badge

*T*he youth athletic programs in New Carrollton, Maryland were among the Washington metro area's finest.

Although I displayed a lot of natural talent in baseball in elementary school, I did not nurture my gifts. Instead, I focused narrowly on academics, music, and scouts.

By seventh grade, I fell behind the other boys who had played on teams, which hurt my self-image and frustrated me from completing personal fitness merit badge, which was required to become an Eagle Scout. Even though I earned more merit badges than anyone, sports had for me become a besetting fear.

Troop 1022 never had an Eagle Scout; why should I expect to be the first? I thought.

On television one afternoon I saw an interview with Dr. Kenneth Cooper, who served as a medical doctor in the Air Force and wrote a fitness book, *Aerobics*, modeled after the paint-by-the-numbers art kits popular at the time.

"Any exercise can be used to become fit so long as one earns twenty exercise points by the end of the week," Dr. Cooper said.

Jogging, swimming, and biking earned more points than other exercises so I decided to take up jogging.

The first day that I jogged in gym class, I ran around the goal posts six or seven times before my physical education teacher stopped me.

"Stephen, is something wrong?"

"No. I am training for personal fitness merit badge."

Later when I jogged down Good Luck Road, a driver pulled over.

"Do you need a ride?"

While everyone knew about running in the context of track and field events, most of the training took place on athletic fields, not on city streets, and involved high school or college athletes. Jogging did not fit the expected context for running and most people worked hard to avoid such manual labor.

My jogging gave me the self-confidence to complete the requirements for personal fitness merit badge and brought me a step closer to earning my Eagle Scout badge. It also helped me overcame a dumpy self-image, and advanced my personal discipline. As time passed, I found that jogging made me aware of God's presence and it became an occasion for prayer.

The Camera

*I*n the fall of 1967 at age fourteen, I set a goal of traveling to Philmont Scout Ranch in New Mexico and committed myself to carrying the Daily News to earn the money needed. I was unsure whether or not I could handle a daily paper route because all of the guys I knew with daily paper routes seemed older and tougher than I was. I also had serious doubts that I could earn enough money to pay for travel, camp expenses, and the required gear.

In spite of my besetting fears, I earned more than enough money to pay my trip expenses. With money left over, I bought a Minolta range-finder, 35 mm camera. This new camera opened my eyes to the visual universe, especially the evening news on television.

Video clips of Vietnam entered our living room every evening at six. On the news, we saw dead bodies laid out, villages burned, and GIs jumping out of helicopters under enemy fire. War scenes became as normal as *Hamburger Helper* and *JELL-O* pudding, blunting my aversion to murder and death.

But, when the Viet Cong launched the Tet Offensive in January 1968, we experienced a new normal. Tet exposed American military invincibility as a myth. The aura of victory in the

Second World War faded flat—no one mouthed the words, but everyone saw the horrible images non-stop, every night on the news. And every night we witnessed GIs dying in a war that no one understood, no one wanted, and no one knew how to end. It shocked me how impotent our leaders became in the face of the horrors of war and I grew cynical about the claims they made.

By March of 1968 President Lyndon Baines Johnson, better known as LBJ, resigned from the fall election.

"If nominated, I will not run; if elected, I will not serve," LBJ said citing William Tecumseh Sherman.

His speech shocked everyone and transformed a sleepy presidential election into a horse race, but the war went on.

Cynicism reached a peak during the coming months of the election. I was too young to vote, but I handed out flyers at the county fair in Upper Marlboro for Richard Nixon—the peace candidate who claimed to have a secret plan to end the war. When Nixon picked Maryland Governor, Ted Agnew, as his running mate we watched with great pride as our governor was chosen. When they won the election, we believed that the war would soon end, but instead the pace of war increased as Nixon initiated a more intense bombing campaign of North Vietnam and enemy supply lines in Cambodia.

At that point in my life, I aspired to become a fighter pilot studying military history, aviation, and navigation. But as the war wore on, I felt increasingly torn between my ambitions to become a military pilot and my religious beliefs. If the United States cared so much about Vietnam, then why did Congress and the President limit military options in the war? If this was a just war, then why were so many religious leaders protesting? Nothing about this *dirty little war* made sense because I believed America to be a liberator, not a colonizer.

While the evening news demonstrated the power in photographs and film, I focused my camera on candid shots of friends and family. In earning a photography merit badge, I learned to develop film, which led me to concentrate on taking black and white pictures that I could edit and crop to perfection. Peace and serenity were my themes. Many of my photographs featured friends peering out of sunlit windows with a background of the green oaks outside our church.

Open windows symbolized the freedom that I felt hiking and camping in the great outdoors, even in the dead of winter. It was like the freedom we experience in Jesus Christ to enjoy life in spite of circumstances. Freedom to pray at any time; freedom to live with purpose and boundaries that we can trust; freedom knowing that the future belongs in Christ and we are his.

Sammi, the youth director at Riverdale Presbyterian church, noticed my interest in photography and invited me to photograph the annual youth group retreat, scheduled in June at a camp on the Chesapeake Bay. To prepare, I purchased plenty of color film (most people considered black and white photography old fashioned) and I studied retreat plans to know who, what, and when to photograph.

While I focused on the technical side of photography, Sammi saw the camera as a way to get me more involved in the youth group. In general, photography challenged me to engage more deeply with the people around me much like video on the evening news challenged me to become more deeply involved in national politics.

As for Philmont, I remember Philmont, not for the pictures, not for the bears, not for the sore feet, but for a radio broadcast that we listened to from the steps of a ranger station on top of a mountain in New Mexico on July 20th. That day when astronauts Neil Armstrong and Buzz Aldrin took the first steps on the moon, something I will never forget.

The Daily Roster

*B*efore young people can go off and conquer the world, they must learn to walk, talk, and take care of themselves. One of the rites of passage along the way is summer camp. If you are a Boy Scout, the camp to end all camps is Philmont Scout Ranch in Cimarron, New Mexico.

Philmont exceeds expectations. Philmont Scout Ranch consists of two-hundred and fourteen square miles of almost pristine wilderness—mountains and ranchland and woods—in the northern New Mexico donated from 1938 to 1942 to the National Council of the Boy Scouts of America (BSA) by oil tycoon Waite Phillips. The ranch contains historical gold mines, outlaw hideouts, Apache and Ute Indian heritage sites, a B-24 crash site, dinosaur excavation sites, and the hunting lodges of the rich and famous. The wildlife includes scorpions, tarantulas, freshwater fish, eagles, rattlesnakes, deer, elk, coyote, antelope, mountain lion, buffalo, beaver, wild turkey, and bear. Philmont is not just another summer camp.

Philmont tests the Scout Motto: *Be Prepared.*

Gathering firewood by myself one evening about a hundred yards from our campsite, I found a deer carcass freshly torn into bloody pieces, which reminded me of the camp rule against walking alone in the woods. During our eleven days in July 1968, we had many other challenges. We saddled Harlan's burros, rode horses, shot skeet, forded the Cimarron River, repelled down Cimarroncito's rock ledges, experienced midnight bear raids, and walked five hundred feet into the Cyphers gold mine, turning the lights out when we got there. We sought to do manly things and Philmont obliged.

Philmont also amplified the problems that we brought with us. As duly elected crew leader, I coordinated daily schedules which included putting up and taking down tents; gathering firewood; acquiring and often purifying water; and cooking meals. We were experienced scouts and during a shakedown backpacking trip near Catoctin Mountain in Maryland, everyone worked well together without supervision. Five days into Philmont, however, the teamwork started breaking down—scouts started malingering and rebelled against my efforts to coordinate work assignments. I drew up a roster to allocate camp duties equitably and salvage unit cohension, but the damage to my authority proved irreparable.

Adding to my difficulties, backpacking aggravated an old back injury. Several years earlier at Ocean City, Maryland I had surfed ocean waves on an inflatable mattress successfully until

I caught a large wave, my mattress got too far in front of it, and I fell head first over the top. I landed on my face and the wave threw my legs over my head. I was paralyzed for several minutes as the surf pounded me under water and I had no strength to get up. Coming to my senses, I slowly crawled out of the water on my stomach. No one saw me laying there; no one came running.

After several days of backpacking at Philmont, my back gave out and intense pain accompanied every footstep. The adults debated helicoptering me out because I had become a liability for the team and the guys resented having to slow down and wait for me. Harsh weather spurred their contempt—the late afternoon thunder-showers brought freezing rain which soaked us and our gear, should we arrive late at our destination and fail to pitch tents promptly. The stress of the long days of the rigorous backpacking and the skimpy trail meals brought out the worst in people and even family friends on my crew ridiculed me harshly for the remainder of the trip.

My dreams of Western adventure and my concepts of self-sufficiency devolved into a struggle to survive and dependence on my team. Nothing I could say; nothing I could do, could make up for the burden I posed. Through the grace of God and my team's support, I hiked out with them.

Once we reached base camp, we discovered the Tooth Of Time Traders Commissary where we found the belts, belt buckles, jackets, and patches that allowed us to brag about our Philmont experiences upon returning home. I quickly forgot the stresses of the trail that for eleven days removed the thin veneer off of civilized society. Still, I never forgot my experience of vulnerability and the usefulness of a duty roster.

The Owl

*I*n eleventh grade I wanted to learn to type. I envied my father who, having typed his dissertation on an Underwood Manual, could type letters using all the proper keystrokes. By contrast, I could only hunt and peck on a typewriter like a newbie. Typing had caché; typing was professional; I wanted to learn to type.

Parkdale Senior High School offered a typing class for aspiring secretaries in 1971, but excluded students in the college track. When I asked to sign up for a one-semester course, my guidance counselor frowned and enrolled me in the second semester class only after considerable prodding on my part. For the first semester, I reluctantly signed up for note-taking, which proceeded without a hitch but halfway through the semester my counselor informed me that I had been bumped out of the typing class. In its place, I took a psychology class.

Psychology started the next semester with little fanfare. Because psychology had no textbook and required no homework, it was popular with students. We met daily for fifty minutes, sat in a big circle, and just talked about the latest rage in pop psychology—not Dale Carnegie, not B. F. Skinner, but group therapy. In group therapy, everyone got their say and the teacher encouraged us to listen courteously to one another.

Listening proved to be a challenge because I knew few of my fellow students, other than a couple whom I had seen in gym class. The students who were not on the college track got to enroll in the typing and shop classes that my counselor had kept me out of, but many of them dropped out. If psychology had been a college-track class, textbooks and homework would have been required, but expectations here were low. In the end, this class educated me mostly about the class divide in America.

One of my follow students—Larry—stood out. Larry was tall, gruff, and wore work jeans with plaid shirts. Now, I enjoyed plaid shirts myself and took a ration of grief for wearing blue jeans and boots to school before either was fashionable, but Larry also looked mean—like walk down the other side of the street kind of mean. On a bad day I might have been afraid of him.

One day our assignment was to pick the name of a person out of a hat, compare the person with an animal, and explain why the comparison was reasonable.

What was this teacher thinking? I thought.

The potential for embarrassment and derision that a new nickname might pose elicited a sense of panic and read throughout the room. Eyes nervously tracked each student as they picked a name out of the hat. Like a deaf man lip-reading, we watched the expressions on their faces as they read the names.

When Larry picked my name, I tensed up. What would he say? How would I respond?

"Steve reminds me of an owl, being quiet and wise."

With those words, my image of Larry changed. He seemed okay, not mean at all.

Who is this guy? I wondered.

Over the next few weeks, the stranger whom I avoided became a friend whom I knew. Later, when the class ended, I missed seeing and talking with him.

Funny. I have no clue whose name I picked that day.

It's Academic

*D*uring the fall of my senior year, Parkdale started participating in the *It's Academic* show, which aired on NBC Channel 4 in the Washington D.C. metro area. To pick a team, the faculty sponsor—my English teacher—asked the guidance office for the names of Parkdale's top fifteen academic students. Not on that list, I complained to fellow students one day in my English class. Soon thereafter, the television studio hosted an open audition for Parkdale students where anyone who wanted to compete could come and demonstrate their *It's Academic* quiz show prowess.

The audition attracted little attention. Only the top fifteen students and I attended. It consisted of a mock *It's Academic* quiz show where the interviewer posed a question and the first student to raise a hand got to respond. Because incorrect answers triggered no penalty and the interviewer posed pretty basic questions, the winning strategy involved only fast hand-raising and average intelligence. By the end of the audition, I single-handedly answered about ninety percent of the questions, and I was invited to join the team.

My fast hand-raising skills embarrassed the other students—all friends and classmates—who focused on correct answers over fast reflexes. They were among the best and the brightest students I have ever known, but they refused to take risks, much like many tech firms in 1990s that introduced great products only to fail later for ignoring customer needs, changing market conditions, and other mundane business details. After our faculty sponsor announced those chosen for the team, she set up regular, after-school practices to prepare for the show.

Shortly after the team began meeting, I decided to attend Indiana University and my father agreed.

"Stephen, you can attend Indiana, but you need to get a part-time job to help meet expenses."

My father's requirement seemed fair and I found a job selling children's shoes at a shop in Capital Plaza Mall.

The shoe-sales position provided more of an education than I bargained for. The shop specialized in expensive, upscale brands that attracted African American women, who wanted to buy the best, name-brand shoes for their kids. Meanwhile, white women in Prince George's County felt no obligation to buy their kids top-of-the-line foot-ware and bought their kids generic shoes at local discount stores.

While store management typically obsessed about proper fitting of children's shoes, they happily slipped ill-fitting, brand-name shoes on insistent mothers. These managers did a lot things that disturbed me.

It disturbed me the managers refused to let me study on quiet days while we sat around. If I took out a book, they assigned me to sort shoes in the back or to watch the store, while they smoked marijuana in the back room. It also bothered me that when President Nixon announced a price freeze on August 15, 1971 to combat inflation, they immediately raised shoe prices throughout the store. I guess that working in that store bothered me about as much as my studying bothered them.

I earned very little selling children' shoes, but I missed afternoon *It's Academic* team practices and got bumped to the backup team.

When Parkdale debuted on the show, I sat and cheered with an attractive Jewish girl, whom I later invited to the senior prom. Like at the audition, team members waited until they knew the answer before pushing the button. They lost and lost badly to the *"fast, button-pushing cheaters,"* or so they complained.

Joyriding

*G*od has a special place in his heart for drunks and foolish kids," my scoutmaster used to claim.

This is the way he normally introduced another story of reckless driving from his youth. His introduction may have cleverly fit the audience present because our adult leaders often drank a case of Jack Daniels together over the weekend and because we scouts always engaged in more foolishness than we admitted in the presence of the adults. Still, neither the drunks nor the fools that taught me to appreciate the wisdom in my scoutmaster's stories.

One fool in need of mercy, a classmate named Bob, used to invite me joyriding after school senior year with a friend who owned a Plymouth Valiant hand-painted in battlefield camouflage colors—gray, brown, and dark green. Joyriding meant fast driving around the winding back roads in Prince George's County while he regaled us with stories about police chases and other teenage folly. Never mind that fast driving and the old Valiant did not credibly fit in the same story—the stories entertained us and the time passed quickly.

Up to a point, I was the ideal driving student. I read the

driver's education textbook cover to cover and scored grades high enough that the instructor curved class grades against my test scores, as he openly admitted. However, I did less well behind the wheel where the mechanics of driving remained new. Even so, unlike many of my peers who complained loudly about taking the Maryland driver's test multiple times, I passed on the first attempt.

My experience joyriding and my driving class results never seemed to intersect. Oh, I watched the gory videos of highway accidents produced by the Ohio State Police, but a driver's license symbolized adulthood and freedom—and that made nasty accidents in Ohio irrelevant.

This is the 1970s and cars now come equipped with seat beats, like racing car drivers use. I thought.

Being smart, I always buckled up. As a serious student and responsible driver, my parents allowed me to drive the family Vega more often than most of my friends and I seldom abused their trust.

One evening friends set me up with a date and plans to attend a movie in downtown Greenbelt, which was on the other side of Greenbelt Park. The shortcut to Greenbelt lay in taking the unlit, park access road, which curved up and down many wooded hills and provided a perfect night-time roller coaster. To loosen things up, I turned off the head lights and drove the four of us through the park in the dark with my friends screaming the entire way.

I enjoyed the movie, but when my date left me to sit with the other two it became obvious that my role for the evening was more as chauffeur and less as eligible bachelor. Hurt and offended, on the way home my disgust grew to the point that I took off my seat belt and let the Vega seat-belt alarm buzz. It buzzed and buzzed and buzzed to the distress of my companions and to my own delight.

Since then, I have given up joyriding and almost always buckle my seat belt. Still, on good days and bad our lives depend, not with our own skill or wisdom or seat belts, but on God's grace and protection.

The Art and Joy of Reading

*D*uring summer vacations in grade school, my sister, Diane, and I competed at my father's urging to see who could read the most books. I loved reading the *Hardy Boys* and the *Lone Ranger* series, and made frequent trips to the library and local used book stores to find books in the series that I had not yet read.

In the fall of my senior year in high school (1971), I took an honors history course with Mrs. C. where I earned college credit, attended seminars at the University of Maryland, and struggled to complete the class reading list. While some took the reading list more seriously than others, a few friends skipped the readings, made up fanciful book titles to justify imaginative conclusions to their papers, and openly joked about it in class. Because I had worked so hard to complete the readings, this cheating offended my sensibilities.

After Mrs. C. gave me a B for the class, I complained about the cheaters. She never confronted the cheaters, but changed my grade to an A for having completed the readings.

The readings for this class challenged my limited understanding of history, but I plodded through them anyway. Over time, I learned to read on two levels. On the surface level, I read for narrative content, facts, and dates. On a deeper level, however, I read to see how the author uses facts and dates to argue his case. Did the author, for example, make a convincing argument or did the author leave out important points inconsistent with the argument?

In the same way, the physical world forms a facade over spiritual realities. We experience revelations from God through daily experiences, prayer, and the spoken word, but most often through reading the Bible.

While none of this came to me in grade school when I started reading or in high school when I learned to study, my love of reading and learning new things inspired a lifelong journey. Later, when I started writing down my reflections and praying over them, life just made more sense.

A Dank Sunrise

*A*t the end of my junior year in high school, our senior pastor retired and the session fired our youth director, leaving the assistant pastor to manage both the church and the youth group, while a new pastor was recruited. Most of our friends found him boring and left, leaving Jon and I as a remnant of the group.

Consequently, my first small group consisted of the two of us and the pastor. The three of us met on Wednesday afternoons for pizza and soda during my senior year to discuss the Apostle Paul's Letter to Romans and Dietrich Bonhoeffer's *The Cost of Discipleship*. In particular, I remember Bonhoeffer's comments on cheap grace:

> *Cheap grace is the preaching of forgiveness without requiring repentance, baptism without church discipline, communion without confession, absolution without personal confession. Cheap grace is grace without discipleship, grace without the cross, grace without Jesus Christ, living, and incarnate (44–45).*

While God sovereignly works in our lives to bring us to faith, we must also embrace and nurture it.

Jon embraced and nurtured his faith in college, but I initially took a different path. Because the youth group provided my primary social activity outside of school, I became deeply bitter about the group's dissolution.

The essay below, *A Dank Sunrise,* won second place in a 1972 Parkdale Senior High School literary contest and remains one of the oldest examples of my writing. The somber tone of this piece anticipated my walk in the desert during the years to follow in college.

> *Cold rain plummets through a dense veil of vibrating pines to shatter against lichen covered stone, lost on a forgotten mountain ridge abandoned by time to grow into dust. Soil-braced rock remains silent listening to the moaning of each pine-spiced bead contributing its loneliness to a stream of tears. An unforgiving wind shuffles a dull mist among the evergreens as it hastens to a distant shower. Splinter white limbs lie shivering, raped by an early winter ice storm in this dark season.*
>
> *Propped up beneath an apex of lifeless stone with his back adjacent to a leafless white oak, an unstirring youth sits staring into the bleak environment. An inanimate individual, he is prodded by the dank sunrise to awaken. Untouched by the selfish wind, his eyes are open solely to the wetting of the pounding rain: yet they speak of a unique pilgrimage, a venture into the soul.*
>
> *In the fluid sunlight of a late May morn, Tamen clears the soft brown hair from his eyes as he wanders into the low thick blueberry and shaggy laurel of a woodland pasture. A pair of head-bobbing*

turtle doves takes wing disturbed by the passing of the inquiring stranger near their hidden perch in the underbrush. Tamen is attracted to a small hillside clearing by a myriad of bright-colored insects producing the resonance of a crafted lute. Wading among the flowering blue-green grasses with a warm breeze bathing his tanned face, he uncovers a path well scored with radiant-textured dandies and winding raspberries leading up the life-lit meadow into the pines.

Over fallen timber, across dry rock ledges, and through clear scented mountain runs, the peaceful path leads Tamen through remnants of quieter times when wise men hoed the fields together and hunted with each other in the woodlands in preparation for the clouded seasons. Below whistling caverns and whispering white pine, he passes experiencing the unselfish melodies of nature's conscience which has been unheard by generations of self-isolated men. Up the mountain's slope to the ridge, the beauteous trail terminates in the reflections of the mineral water of a crystal pool.

The cool serenity of the pool invites the sojourner to relax securely at the water's skirt. Peering down with the expressive innocence of an infant at play, Tamen is attentive to the life-painted images dancing on the wavering liquid. In its reflections he sees an unfamiliar child skipping alone in the March sunlight on a field of fresh-green rye grass. First in silent amazement, then with tears in his eyes, Tamen watches the shining adolescent grow in life into a man of his own image. Tamen, awakened in this natural solitude, is quiet with himself.

a window opens	*clouds thicken*
light implodes	*motion freezes*
ice melts	*a crow sings*

Our dessert walks are as much a part of our Christian journey as our mountaintop experiences. When Moses went to Pharaoh, he repeatedly asked: "*Let my people go, that they may serve me in the wilderness.*" (Exod 7:16) It was in the desert that the Patriarchs learned to serve God and so must we. Even the experience of nihilism points to God because the human heart refuses to live without hope.

Vietnam

One of the oldest books on my bookshelf is L. E. Moore's *Elementary Aviation* (1943), which teaches pilots the rudiments of navigation, such as flying on instruments, meteorology, and radio navigation. I purchased this book in a second-hand bookstore in junior high school because I wanted to attend the Air Force Academy and become a pilot. When I learned that my eyesight disqualified me for pilot's training, I joined a Sea Explorer's unit and set my sights on the Naval Academy. My interest in the military academies continued into high school, when I began running cross country in 1970 knowing that the academies expected cadets to be athletes and the military also had physical training requirements.

My friends noticed my fascination with the military. At a Boy Scout camporee, one friend in high school nicknamed me: *"The General"*; afterward, when he learned that I had joined the Sea Explorers, he revised my nickname to: *"The Admiral"*. True to my nickname, I worked as an aquatics instructor at Camp Ross, one of six Boy Scout camps in Goshen, Virginia, for two summers where I taught swimming, rowing, and canoeing. I also attended seamanship classes offered on Saturday mornings at the Navy Yard in Washington D.C.

Although my father had attended the reserved officer training corps (ROTC) and served in Korea, he discouraged my interest in flying, disparaging the pilot's job as a type of *"bus service in the sky."* Although he expressed his feelings on the subject, he also made it clear that I needed to sort out my career aspirations for myself.

The evening news prompted my doubts about military service. Video clips from Vietnam dominated the evening news for years, but progress in ending the war seemed illusive. World War II lasted for five years and involved battles all over the world so why did this little *"police action"* in Vietnam take longer?

The usual answer to this question was that communism was inherently evil and required determined opposition. Communists in Europe and Asia had murdered millions of their own citizens to implement totalitarianism (commonly referred to as a *"dictatorship of the proletariat"*) and promoted state-sponsored atheism and the persecution of Christians. Even today this sordid history boggles the mind, but in the rush to condemn lesser evils we seldom hear much about it.

Defending South Vietnam from a communist takeover therefore seemed consistent with the Christian concept of a just war, but the prosecution of the war that we witnessed in the evening news did not seem just. Why the massacre at Mi Lai? Why the summary execution of Viet Cong prisoners?

While such questions lingered in my mind, the carnage on the evening news educated me to the reality of modern war. To my 18-year-old eyes, indiscriminate bombing, routine use of napalm, and relocation of civilians appeared shocking, provocative, un-American. Noble ends do not justify ignoble means.

Questions about the Vietnam War already colored my thinking in 1968 when I campaigned for Richard Nixon along with my parents because he proposed a plan to the end the war. But my attitude about military service and the Naval Academy remained positive until my junior year, when my Christian faith and my aspirations to serve in the military began to feel disconnected.

This disconnect came to a head on August 4, 1972 when I wrote to my draft board in applying for I-0 status as a conscientious objector:

> *I cannot fight in a war because as a Christian my highest duty is to follow the teachings of Jesus Christ. I believe that life is to be honored and respected by all men as a sacred gift of God. I believe that every man has a constructive contribution to make to humanity and that each man has the right to fulfill this destiny. I believe there is a beauty in all life and that we should use love, concern, and*

non-violent methods to solve our conflicts. I believe
all men are of one indivisible whole and that each
man's life is important to the life of the whole. I
must live in peace to uphold my faith.

I wrote as a pacifist because I did not fully understand just war theory. I could support a just war, but Vietnam was a colonial war, which we learned much later.

My draft board classified me as I-0, which exempted me from military service. However, they required me to take the usual military medical examination and find alternative service to perform, if and when they called my draft number (13).

My medical examination took place in Indianapolis in the fall of 1972. During the exam, every registrant classified I-0 in the room was asked to stand up. Among the several hundred registrants present, I stood alone.

In the fall of my freshman year in college, I wrote to public interest research groups around the country inquiring about job prospects that might satisfy my alternative service requirement. A group in Baltimore, Maryland, responded to my inquiry, but the war officially ended on December 31, 1972 and the draft board never called my number. Because draft numbers up to 153 had been called the previous year, I took the war's end as God's gracious provision.

COLLEGE

The Audition

*I*n high school in the fall of 1971, I pooled my resources and bought a new Conn 88h trombone. As a base trombone, the Conn 88h differed visibly from the tenor trombone, a used Silver Bach Stradivarius built in the 1930s that I had played since the fifth grade. The Conn 88h had a Remington mouthpiece, a trigger for outer register notes, and a distinctive, mellow sound. Shortly after getting my new trombone, I auditioned and won a coveted first chair in the Prince George's County Youth Orchestra and I began practicing an hour a day.

During my last two years of high school, I also played first chair in both the Parkdale Symphonic Band and the school orchestra. During my senior year, I was one of the few instrumentalists who enrolled in the music composition class or competed in county and state solo competitions. Meanwhile, at Riverdale Presbyterian Church, I sang in the Youth Choir and took voice lessons from the choir director. I also took private lessons from the tubist with the National Symphony Orchestra. My favorite photograph from senior year shows me performing in a jazz ensemble with *"shades,"* which suggests how much music meant to me.

Music played an important role in my social life and I enjoyed modest success as a player. Music also taught me personal discipline and served as a metaphor for God's presence in my life.

At one point, I became aware of my lack of Sabbath rest in the midst of many commitments and deadlines. I prayed to God that he allow me to keep the Sabbath—to rest with Him—as I slept. God honored that prayer and reminded me by waking me to the sound of joyous music in my mind's ear.

I started to consider music as a career possibility. As I prepared to apply to colleges in the fall of 1971, I announced to my parents, friends, and teachers that I planned to audition for the Indiana University School of Music in Bloomington, Indiana.

The seriousness of my decision to audition for music school remained unclear at that point, either in terms of the talent or the commitment required. College seemed a long way off so I assumed, naively, that picking a course of study in high school allowed plenty of time to prepare. While this assumption might have been true for academic majors, music required a higher level of preparation.

My private teacher expressed concern about my preparation for this audition, perhaps observing that music was more of a social activity than a professional aspiration in my life. Professional musicians practice many hours a day to reach a level of perfection seldom attained by amateurs. I had only recently moved from half an hour to an hour of practice daily, an insufficient level of commitment for an aspiring professional.

By year end, I started practicing closer to two hours a day and my teacher arranged for me to study with a colleague of his, a trombonist with the National Symphony Orchestra. The new instructor adjusted my embouchure to account for my overbite, which would eventually help me play with a wider range in the upper register, but initially it reduced my performance range. The new, more vigorous practice schedule, embouchure change, and new teacher excited and overwhelmed me as I prepared to audition.

Also overwhelmed was my father, who saw music as a great hobby, but doubted that my modest talent could blossom into a viable career. He had confidence that my audition would lead the music department at Indiana University to reach the same conclusion. We agreed that, if I passed the audition, I could study music, but if I failed it, I would accept the result and focus my studies elsewhere.

When the time came to audition in January 1972, I traveled alone to Bloomington, Indiana on a Friday and stayed that night in a dormitory. A friend, who studied viola and whom I had met the previous summer at a church retreat, invited me to dinner in the cafeteria and introduced me to some music students. Tired from the trip, after dinner I took a shower and went to bed.

On Saturday morning, I walked over to the music building early to warm up. After warming up, I waited with students coming and going—horns blowing, strings playing, flutes piping—as auditions ran late. Jazzed up, overstimulated, and anxious beyond words, when my turn to play arrived, I was unable to play a Bb scale. Having given the judges no reason to pass me, I failed the audition.

When I returned home, I remained active in the music program in high school and spent the spring preparing for a July concert tour in Europe with the Parkdale Symphonic Band. Meanwhile, I accepted admission at Indiana University and prepared to enter as a freshman without a major.

The Detour

When the pickup slowed and the driver looked over at me, I saw only the shotgun on the gun rack. He pulled over ahead of me, got out, and waved me over to the side of the road. I slowed my bicycle and stopped behind the pickup, leaning on one foot—three hundred miles from home, off my route, and all alone, I felt vulnerable—scared that I might end up like the two bikers in Easy Rider—shot-gunned to death. Rather than motorcycling drugs from California to Florida, in August 1972 I cycled from Washington D.C. to start college in Indiana.

"Why did you leave Route 50?"

This guy had obviously followed me down Route 19 from Clarksburg, I thought.

"The sign on Route 50 forbids bicycles west of Bridgeport," I answered.

Actually, where Route 50 divided into a four-lane highway, a big, green sign with white letters read: PEDESTRIANS, BICY-CLES, MOTOR-DRIVEN CYCLES—PROHIBITED.

"I hoped to detour south to Route 119 where I can continue west," I continued.

"We had ten bicyclists ride through here last week. Nobody cares about that sign."

"Really? Thanks for the tip." I said, as the driver returned to his pickup.

This gun-rack angel saved me from a difficult detour and perhaps an extra day's travel, I thought as he drove off. Studying my traffic map, I wished that I had a topographical map showing the West Virginia mountains that separated Route 19 from Route 50. I could see that local roads could be used to jog over to Route 50 at Salem, about eighteen miles off—as the crow flies—but the quality of the roads remained murky.

Typical challenge that Eagle Scouts enjoy. I thought.

With a yucca backpack slung over the handlebars, I cycled up Route 33 that cuts off of Route 19, also called Milford Street, along Sycamore Creek. As the road ascended uphill into the woods, the grading became progressively rougher. Pavement gave way to gravel, which gave way to dirt which gave way to stones, which gave way to transmission-eating boulders, where I had to walk the bike. Walking through shaded, old-growth oaks among the boulders, at least gave relief from the morning heat.

After crossing a creek the grading improved and I passed tin-roofed shacks—not abandoned, not maintained, just depressing—and I found myself in the Appalachia mentioned on television only during election years and then only in passing.

"Where y'a headed?" A local asked.

He must have questioned my sanity as I panted up the hill that morning on a three-speed bike built mostly for city streets.

My thoughts wandered, focused partly on the war—far off in Southeast Asia, yet ever-present in political rallies, school discussions, and family feuds. Would my draft board grant my request for 1-0 status as a conscientious objector? If granted, where would I work? If denied, how would I respond?

As I stained up this seemingly endless hillside, I walked more than peddled. By my fourth day on the road the sunburn no longer bothered me, but I chafed at the ever-present hunger and thirst. Relieving the hunger would have to wait until I returned to a more populated area, but I prayed that my canteen water lasted until I got there.

What a fool I had been, I thought, focusing on a girl who mostly ignored me when I slavishly visited on my first night out at a camp west of Winchester, Virginia. Now that my foolishness had legs, the remainder of the trip—like life itself—seemed pointless and cruel. Late in the morning and graciously before I lost my mind, the hillside peaked at the ridge and the grading upgraded to macadam for the first time since leaving Route 19.

With the ridge, my thoughts quickened. The oak trees,

the dirt road, and Appalachian poverty gave way, like the morning mist in afternoon sun, to neatly grazed bluegrass fields, white boarded fences, and country homes with expansive porches. As my bike picked up speed gliding down the hill, a black lab on one porch perked up and sounded off as he ran down the yard. With my bike accelerating, I paid little attention thinking—what dog can run forty miles an hour? As I picked up speed, I focused more on enjoying the cool breeze than on the dog approaching from behind.

"Grrrrr" growled the dog that snapped at my left foot.

This stupid dog thinks that he can catch me! I thought.

Still accelerating, I moved my left foot over to stand with both feet on the right pedal. The dog had seen that trick before and moved to snap at me on the right side. Still accelerating, I moved both feet back over to the left pedal. Before the dog could respond, the road veered sharply to the left. Being on the left pedal, leaning into the turn or braking was impossible because I was going too fast. In an instant, I ran off the right side of the road into the ditch.

My front wheel slid into a roadside sewer ditch and pitched me over the handlebars. I hit the ground on the other side of the ditch hard—sliding and rolling another twenty or thirty feet. I came to a stop face down: stunned, sweating, speechless. I lay barely conscious with my face in the dirt. No one came running; no one noticed.

Finally, I picked up my head to look around. The dog stood on the road looking at me. When he saw me look up, he wagged his tail, and wandered off. At that point, I smelled the sewage and sat up confused about what happened.

I got up and examined my bike, certain that it had been ruined and was surprised to find only a small dent in the front wheel. I pulled up a few weeds to clean off the sewage, but I could do nothing about the smell.

I don't remember the trip down Route 31 to Route 28 and up to Patterson Fork Road that brought me into Salem, but I do remember the exhaustion, the hunger, and the heat. I also remember the anxious desire to call my parents using my emergency dime. As I drew closer to Salem, however, I resolved to find a restaurant, get cleaned up, and eat lunch before deciding what to do next.

When I found a restaurant, I still felt sorry for myself as I washed up to get rid of the smell. Other senses returned as I enjoyed a fresh-grilled hamburger with fries and a slice of apple pie a la mode. With every bite, I forgot more—more about the foolishness, more about the dog attack, and more about the heat and noxious smell. As time passed, I reflected on the unlikely intervention of the gun-rack angel and remembered my mileage goal for the day. After lunch, I called my parents to report on progress, got back on my bike, and cycled on to Ohio.

INPIRG Volunteer

*F*all registration at Indiana University in my freshman year took place in a large auditorium where the different departments set up tables and students lined up to enroll in classes. Once students enrolled in their classes, we waited in another line to pay our tuition. As I stood in line, a volunteer with the Indiana Public Interest Research Group (INPIRG) encouraged me to check their funding request on the tuition form (one dollar) and invited me to learn more about the group in an organizational meeting later that evening. Intrigued, I checked off INPIRG on my tuition form and attended the meeting, where students elected me to INPIRG's board of directors.

INPIRG was organized by several law students who had been greatly influenced by Ralph Nader and his new book, *Action for a Change: A Student's Manual for Public Interest Organizing*, which outlined the consumer protection goals for a national organization of the student PIRGs, such as INPIRG. Ralph Nader was himself an attorney and famous for his work on consumer rights and automobile safety.

INPIRG soon became my home away from home. As a board member, I chaired the personnel committee which in the fall hired an executive director. As a volunteer, I organized a new bookstore pricing survey which reported on which bookstore offered the best prices at the beginning of each semester and became popular among students because it helped them save money. Other INPIRG projects included a weekly grocery pricing study and work on local utility rates.

My freshman year of college at Indiana University I lived and worked in the (former) Graduate Residence Center (GRC) where almost everyone had a roommate and shared hallway telephones. Because one of the three buildings in GRC housed women, the university advertised it as co-educational.

GRC helped me expand on my work with INPIRG in the spring semester with an independent study of two Indiana state government offices in Indianapolis: the new state regulator of private schools and the state department of weights and measures. Each study involved background reading about the agencies' founding legislation and accomplishments, interviews with state officials and their critics, and lengthy written reports. By the end of the semester, I developed a passion for problem-solving research.

Hitch Hiking

*D*uring spring break in March, 1973, I drove with a wealthy graduate student from Bloomington, Indiana to visit my parents in Maryland. Because he did not plan to return to Bloomington, I decided to visit friends at Harvard University before returning to school. So after a week at home, I got up early one morning, packed my backpack, wrote BOSTON with a magic marker on a sheet of cardboard, and hiked past Riverdale Shopping Center to stand on the north-bound ramp of the Baltimore-Washington Parkway.

I reached the ramp around seven a.m. and by quarter to eight I secured a ride from one of the commuters heading east on the parkway. As I learned from my map, the parkway runs east, parallel with Interstate 95, and after Baltimore merges into 95 which continues to Boston, a trip that normally takes about ten hours.

That morning I thumbed my way to the business district in Philadelphia. I then spent the afternoon traveling from there to New York City and the evening taking short rides to the other side of the city. After standing in the dark for a couple hours, after midnight I left the Interstate, walked over to an apartment building, and slept the night in a heated stairwell. People walking up the stairs occasionally woke me up, but no one gave me a hard time and in the morning I walked over to a nearby restaurant to buy breakfast.

After breakfast I hitch-hiked to Bridgeport, Connecticut where a middle-aged man picked me up, drove me across town, stopped in a lonely place, and parked the car. Here I listened while he sipped coffee, cried, and described a strained relationship with his son. Whenever I interjected anything about my relationship with my own father, he became irritated and defensive.

As time passed, I noticed that he smelled of alcohol and sipped coffer to cover it up, which only increased my anxiousness to reach Cambridge. After he cycled through his concerns several times, he tired of our conversation, drove me to the other side of Bridgeport, and dropped me off. From there, I quickly found a ride to Cambridge and made my way to Harvard.

On campus I stayed at Adams House, where my best friend, Jon, lived in an apartment with three other guys. During my days on campus, we visited the Fox Club, attended several classes together, and took part in a youth program at his church. At the Fox club, I got the full tour, stopping to examine the many stuffed fox heads lining the wall and having lunch. In a history class, the lecture addressed parliamentary events during colonial times taking place in the building where we sat. In an education class, we heard a guest lecture by the producers of Sesame Street, a popular educational television program for young kids. At the church, we played games and talked about faith, focusing on the story of Daniel and the lion's den.

The church discussion proved uncomfortable for me because I struggled with disbelief more than other students and felt myself assuming the role of the lions in the story. More generally, however, I saw the picture of faith being promoted in churches as hopelessly out of touch.

While I struggle to deal with drunken fathers in Bridgeport, the church focuses on children's bed-time stories. I thought.

I simply could not link stories from the past to present meanings at that point in my life.

By the time my visit ended, Harvard had impressed me beyond words and, as I drew a new sign—BLOOMINGTON, INDIANA—in preparing to leave, I reflected on my choice of schools. Harvard's mystique made students feel special and the freshman tutors personalized the university experience. At Harvard, classes were smaller than at Indiana and I hated to return.

As I prepared to leave Cambridge, hot spring days had turned bitter cold and the almost-fashionable, yellow wind-break-er that I wore on the trip up left me frozen. I soon found myself dancing in the cold alongside of the road to keep warm, which amused those driving by but not enough to offer me a ride.

The road trip west from Cambridge proved uneventful until in Connecticut I got picked up by a couple of long-hair, hippy bartenders in a Volkswagen bus on their way to Pittsburgh. After so many short rides and so much energetic dancing, getting a ride to Pittsburgh seemed like a dream come true. Better yet, they claimed to know a woman in Pittsburgh who could put us all up for the night.

When we arrived in Pittsburgh late that afternoon, my bartending hosts showed oddly little interest in calling their friend but, instead, hunted up a bar and started knocking down shot glasses of hard liquor. Afterwards, when we piled back into the VW bus, they drove up an exit ramp and we found ourselves dodging cars as we headed down the wrong side of the highway. After midnight, they finally stopped along the side of the road to ask for directions and another drunk—a lawyer and former University of Maryland basketball player—invited us to his house for the night. After frying up bacon and eggs for us at around two in the morning, the lawyer gave me a room with a bed and I went to sleep.

At seven-thirty in the morning, a small child pulled on my foot and woke me up.

"Daddy, daddy," she said. "Some strange men are sleeping on the couch."

"I am so sorry. Your father is in the other room." I rolled over and responded.

After she left, I woke up the bartenders up.

"We need to go. This guy is going to wake up, not remember anything, and call the cops."

So we left. The bartenders drove me to the west side of Pittsburgh and dropped me off.

The country roads west of Pittsburgh seemed to meander aimlessly and the light local traffic offered only short rides to fill a long day. By evening my last ride dropped me off at a truck stop in Cambridge, Ohio and advised me to hitch a ride with a trucker, who might offer me a lengthier lift.

At the truck stop, I sat at the counter on a stool and ate a welcome dinner of liver, onions, and mashed potatoes with gravy. The guy sitting next to me started up a conversation and, after dinner, he helped me find a trucker traveling west to Indianapolis. His cab had only a driver's seat so I slept uncomfortably on a pile of junk that night, but woke up in Indianapolis the next morning, where we ate breakfast together at a diner.

After breakfast, I met a black student from school and we hitch hiked together south on Route 37 to Bloomington. A local man offered us a ride and entertained us with lively stories as we passed through Martinsville, Indiana.

"A twenty-one year old, black woman named Carol Jenkins," he said, *"tried to sell encyclopedias door-to-door in Martinsville back in 1968 and turned up dead in the street. The police never found her killers but the papers said it was the Klu Klux Klan sending a message to other blacks to stay out of town."*

Whether true or false, the story scared me and petrified my friend. For the remainder of the trip, we sat silently, anxious to get back to campus.

Afterwards, I never hitch hiked again.

Listening and Talking

The stereotype of male-female relations in 1972 followed Dustin Hoffman's film, *The Graduate* (1967), where an older woman seduced a recent high school graduate who later falls in love with her daughter. The only older women in my life taught in the university and, although I became acquainted with many younger women, they preferred older, more experienced guys who could afford to date.

One morning I ran into a female friend, whom I thought I knew better than I did, leaving the room of the guy across the hall, who had a single room.

"Hey, Steve," she said smiling at me.

I said nothing, embarrassed to see her.

Then, the guy came out, saw me, and put on a big grin as he locked his door.

Unable to afford dating freshman year, hanging out with female friends in college seemed unscripted, awkward, and without an obvious social context or meaning—what do you talk about? Real conversation required common values and verbal skills that I lacked.

Over the coming months, I soon discovered an Italian girl in the Graduate Residence Center (GRC) that I had known in high school before her family had moved to Indiana. I also met a Jewish girl from Maryland who I was able to commute home with occasionally over breaks.

One thing that I learned about getting to know people was to ask questions. People love to talk about themselves. You could ask a question and expect conversation to go on for hours. You only needed to speak occasionally to say things like *"yeah"* or *"tell me more."* I grew to love questions and became a good listener.

Later, I learned to ask people about their faith journey.

"What is your favorite scripture passage?"

Or, maybe:

"How did you come to faith?"

It is surprising to see how much you can learn about a person and how quickly.

Dish Machine

*M*y roommate in the Graduate Residence Center (GRC), a business major, looked with a jaundiced eye at my volunteer work as a *"Nader Raider."* An avid golfer, he practiced his putt most evenings in our room and occasionally ganged up with the guy across the hall to play loud music and to bounce a basketball off the door as I prepared for exams.

Following a couple of such incidents, I arranged to move out of GRC and into a single room in the German Language House, where I focused on my volunteer work with Indiana Public Interest Research Group (INPIRG) and my studies, particularly German and comparative literature.

While I enjoyed studying the German language and generally found German literature fascinating, the cynicism in postmodern literature offended my Christian sensibilities, particularly Jesus' admonishment for us to forgive those who sin against us (Matt 6:15). This was the theme of Friedrick Dürrenmatt's play, *The Visit,* that I studied in my sophomore year.

In the play, a rich, old woman returned to her home town and offered the city fathers a generous sum of money with one condition: the town's citizens must kill the man who got her pregnant as a young woman and ran her out of town. At first, people refused this evil request, but over time townspeople convinced themselves that murdering him it was the right thing to do and they killed the man. At this point, the old woman wrote a check for the mayor, placed the man's body in a casket that she brought with her, and left town.

In my distress over such cynicism, I sought refuge from my academic distress by attending dormitory parties. At one such party, I danced with a woman who came from a military family in Virginia. Uncomfortable dancing, she moved like a wooden puppet with frozen joints; I labored to lead and turn her with great effort. Without looking, we twirled around and our locked hands socked my gorgeous German instructor in the face with a thud, giving her a nose bleed.

What do you say to your bleeding instructor? Embarrassed, my dance partner sprinted out of the room, leaving me with the instructor.

My instructor, a married graduate student, dabbed the blood from her nose with a tissue and turned to me.

"Would you like to dance?" She asked.

How could I refuse?

While I enjoyed the parties, they kept me up late Saturday evenings and made it a challenge working the breakfast shift in the cafeteria, which began at six a.m. I volunteered to work on Sunday mornings because hardly anyone got up for breakfast and working the disk washing machine I could normally sleep—nobody knew; nobody cared.

One Sunday morning I woke up with a terrible headache. Smarting from the hangover and distraught over my languishing career as a student, I felt like the prodigal son slopping hogs in a foreign country (Luke 15:17) and realized that I needed to make some changes.

Why Finish College?

*M*y frustration with school during my freshman year prompted me to move out of the German House and into an apartment as I entered my sophomore year in the fall. I also started looking for work that did not require a college degree.

One job I considered was to work full-time for the Indiana Public Interest Research Group (INPIRG), where I had volunteered as an organizer serving community groups in west Bloomington. This area received scant attention from local politicians because it lay in poor neighborhoods on the other side of the railroad tracks.

One community group expressed concerns about a burned-out house on the edge of town that remained as fire-fighters had left it—a partially burned down structure with broken glass and a flooded basement. Neighborhood parents worried about this house because their kids used the abandoned structure as a playground and floated on inner-tubes in the filthy basement water.

I documented these concerns with eight-by-ten inch, black and white photographs which I took with me in a visit with city officials, who showed little interest.

"We can't do anything about this problem. The owners had abandoned the property and, besides, it is located outside the city limits." The city attorney told me.

He then proceeded to lecture me about the need for better childcare among the concerned parents. Because officials expressed indifference and all the poor neighborhoods fell conveniently outside the city limits, I later led a community demonstration in front of city hall and brought a delegation to appear before the next city council meeting, where I made my first television appearance on the local channel.

When INPIRG announced plans to hire a full-time community organizer, I hoped to elevate my volunteer effort to full-time work. But, after I interviewed for the position, they hired someone else, which left me feeling betrayed and unappreciated.

I also tried working with telemarketing for a local police organization. The work consisted of sitting in a room around a table with a bank of telephones and calling everyone in the telephone book, one after another. With each call, they instructed us to ask for the man of the house, assuming that men would more likely identify with a police organization and offer donations. This instruction proved difficult, however, because many elderly widows lived in the community and would break out crying when you asked for the man of the house. After about a week of tearful phone calls, I quit.

As frustrating as college had been, working with INPIRG and in the community taught me that life outside of school could also be frustrating. I became despondent that I had no serious alternative to remaining in college.

As the son of an economist, I knew how to succeed in economics and my work in INPIRG unleased a passion for research. Consequently, even though I had never taken an economics class, I resolved to study economics and to transfer to another school, where I would have fewer distractions.

Return to the Commonwealth

*A*t the end of my sophomore year, I returned to the Commonwealth of Virginia where I worked construction and attended summer school at William and Mary College. In the fall, I transferred to Iowa State University beginning in the winter quarter.

During these months, I worked at a number of job sites where work could be found by asking the foreman on the site. I helped lay pipe in an eight-story, apartment building called the McLean House; I did general labor to help construct the Mitre Building in Tyson's Corner; I picked apples for a couple weeks in Vermont; and I helped both a carpenter and a painter in McLean.

Most of co-workers grew up in West Virginia, much like the colorful character who was my boss at the Mitre site. Most weekends he drank and played poker on Fridays until the paychecks earned that week had disappeared. One weekend he returned to West Virginia, got liquored up, and shot up a friend's trailer, ending up in jail. On weekdays, he found other ways to make trouble.

One day as he and I looked out the window and watched a worker doing wheelies with a Bobcat in the parking lot.

"You know," he told me, *"I told that guy yesterday that you said he was a wimp."*

I about passed out on the spot, but later realized that he was just teasing me again.

I also worked with two African American guys from Washington D.C.—one noisy and one quiet. The noisy one bragged loudly about being a kind of Leroy Brown, which I found amusing. I teased him until he pulled out a razor and chased me around the room. The quiet one never said anything, but one evening he robbed a bank at gunpoint and the next morning the police cordoned off our building hoping to capture him when he showed up at work, which he never did.

The threat of gun and knife violence was part and parcel of work at these construction sites. One painter's helper who I worked alongside from West Virginia refused to horse around with me but routinely horsed around with other country boys.

"Why don't you mess around with me like the other guys?" I asked him one morning.

"You college boys are dangerous," he told me. *"When a misunderstanding arises, you think that you need to get a gun involved."*

Our boss also talked about guns a lot and routinely

brought a pistol to work on paydays. After he cheated me out of about twenty dollars on payday, I understood why.

By October, I had earned enough money working construction to buy my first car, a baby blue, 1967 Volkswagen beetle. While I enjoyed owning a car, the pain and agony that went into earning the money to buy this old car seemed way out of proportion to the joy that it brought. Crazy as they were, my work experiences helped me understand and appreciate the value of a college education and I never again seriously considered dropping out of school.

After Thanksgiving, I started school at Iowa State University in Ames, Iowa. Iowa State's internationally-recognize program in agricultural economics interested me and Ames was close enough to Oskaloosa that I could drive down to visit my grandparents on weekends.

Navigators

My lack of church attendance posed no problem when I was away at Indiana University, but it became a source of friction when I returned home for holidays and summer vacation. Because my parents moved from Maryland to Virginia during my freshman year, I lost touch with most of my high school friends and the kids my age in Virginia were too busy with their own friends to pay much attention to me. Between the local cliques and my own bitterness, I had no reason to attend church beyond the prompting of my parents.

Reflecting on my reasons for avoiding the church, I realized that although I bitterly objected to the leadership of the church who had fired my youth director at Riverdale Presbyterian Church, I still believed in God. My relationship with the church and with God had to be separated. With this obstacle to my faith journey removed, I was able to experience God's presence again both in and out of the church.

God's presence can be found almost anywhere, because the human heart refuses to live without hope. Even as I walked in the desert in college struggling with the cynical world around me, as an intellectual I had to experience God both relationally and logically.

Logically, I found God's presence in Pascal's Wager convincing. Pascal argued that faith was a fair bet because if God exists and you believe, then you win heaven, but if God does not exist and you believe, then you lose nothing. Putting these two things together, the probability of God's existence is a sure thing.

Relationally, my attitude about church attendance began to change after I transferred in my junior year to Iowa State University in Ames, Iowa. In 1974, I spent Christmas break with my grandparents in Oskaloosa, Iowa and celebrated the holidays at Central Reformed Church. After that, I visited them occasionally on weekends and joined them for church before returning to school.

I also shared a room in Wilson Hall with Dennis who introduced me to the Navigators, a campus Christian group, and took me to his church on Sunday. The Navigators had picnics and other events around campus that I attended occasionally to get to know other students.

Dennis attended a nondenominational church that featured praise music and readings from the *Living Bible,* which did not appeal to me. After a few weeks at Dennis' church, I felt a need to continue attending church, but I began attending Collegiate Presbyterian Church (CPC), whose choral music and use of the Revised Standard Version of the Bible were more familiar. Back in the 1950s, I later learned, my parents also attended CPC.

Economic History

*D*uring my last two years of college, I took a series of classes in economic history to further my understanding of economic development, which is more of an historical process than economists typically admit. Understanding this process helps explain why some poor countries have prospered while others, even with better resources, languished in poverty.

Modern economics began with the writings of Adam Smith, who held a chair in moral philosophy at the University of Glasgow, in Scotland. Today Smith would have taught theology in a seminary department of ethics. Think of price theory as weighing the goodness (revenue) and badness (cost) of a product to determine its moral standing (profitability). While most economists today are atheists, if you believe that all knowledge is God's knowledge (Prov 1.7), then Adam Smith's background in moral philosophy makes perfect sense.

Unfortunately, economic history often made little sense to me and my history professor showed no interest in helping me understand why.

"If you sign up with the next class in this sequence, I will flunk you," he told me, tired of my questions.

I had no reason to doubt his warning, but I took it as a

challenge.

After working unsuccessfully to please him with several papers, I went into his office and sat on his desk until he explained the problem, which boiled down to a philosophical difference. I assumed history to be a chronological narrative of events, while he approached history through the eyes of deductive reasoning, which mandated that papers should state a hypothesis and prove it with historical observations. When I used this procedure in my next paper, he liked it. After that point, I paid close attention to philosophical differences and methods of argumentation in all my classes.

The same philosophical differences came up again in a graduate level macro-economic class during my senior year. The economics department at Iowa State focused on teaching and using quantitative methods (deductive methods), but my macro-economics professor preferred a history of thought method of argumentation (chronological argumentation). The tension between these two methods set him at odds with the department and his abrasive personality aggravated the situation—sixteen of the twenty students who signed up for his class dropped it. I stuck it out and earned a B.

Methodological flexibility later served me well professionally, setting me apart from philosophically rigid colleagues and becoming a theme in my writing. In seminary, methodological flexibility helped me to understand and apply various methods of biblical interpretation.

Sharp divisions in the church today are rooted in how scripture is interpreted. Can a sociological critique be used to interpret the Bible or must the interpretation focus on the author's intent, historical context, and other scripture? While many people dismiss interpretive methods as too theological, failure to understand them has led to a lot of unnecessary disagreements.

Senior Year Transition

*M*y senior year at Iowa State, I confidently registered for eighteen credit hours to prepare for graduate studies. I took graduate level micro and macro-economic classes plus undergraduate classes in economic history, computer science, and statistics. On top of my class load, I worked in the cafeteria and played inter-mural basketball.

My floor in Wilson Hall had an excellent basketball team because most of my buddies played varsity-level basketball in high school. But if I felt out of their league playing basketball with small town guys, the small town girls proved equally difficult to get to know. Unlike the movie stereotypes of rural kids dying to get out of their small towns, these kids remained intensely loyal to their hometowns and chose careers and friends that allowed them to return there. As an out-of-state student, breaking into these local high school cliques proved challenging.

In my micro-economics class that fall, I met a bright young Zoroastrian girl from Iran and I invited her to a live production of the musical, *1776*, at the Stephens Auditorium across the street from her dormitory. On the evening of our date, I put on my best clothes, and proudly went down to my car to drive over to her place. When I turned the key to start up the car, sparks flew, smoke emanated from the engine, and the car refused to start—someone had re-arranged the spark-plug wires on the engine to my Volkswagen Beetle. Too late to make other arrangements, I jogged the two miles over to my date's dormitory and arrived a sweaty mess, but she never said a word about it despite her well-developed sense of fashion.

We dated for several months, but she always poked fun at my car. Like most Iranian women, she had assumed that, like most Middle Eastern families, my father would naturally buy me a better car for graduation. I proudly defended my car, having paid for it myself, and took her assumptions about my family situation as biting criticism. Her criticism ultimately cut too deeply for my fragile ego to accept and we broke up.

Physical exhaustion no doubt contributed to my sensitivity about the car. During senior year, I rose at six in the morning to work the breakfast shift in the cafeteria, attended classes all day, and I studied until eleven at night. Then, I went jogging to wake up and worked until around two in the morning. Sleeping only about four hours a night during the week, I took caffeine pills to stay awake and cat-napped during the day when I could. While I attended church that year, I did not otherwise practice Sabbath rest.

In January 1976, I applied to three graduate schools recommended by my father that had strong agricultural economic programs: University of Massachusetts, Iowa State University, and Cornell University. Each offered me admission and financial support, but I preferred Cornell, an Ivy League school closer to home.

By May the stress and long hours pushed me to the breaking point and I got sick. When the student clinic diagnosed me with mononucleosis, I freaked out. My history professor's assistant happened to be in the clinic at the time and she took off running to tell him the news. For a full-time student, mononucleosis might as well have been the plague. In the dormitory, my roommate and friends shunned me, leaving me to eat and study alone.

"Finish up your classes," my dad advised, *"and I will pick you up after a business trip I have to Des Moines later in May."*

The couple of weeks that I had until my father's trip proved about right. Iowa State had a rule that a graduating senior with a B average or better was exempted from final examinations, which dramatically cut my workload. I had already written my term papers for the quarter, which left the remaining weeks for examinations and class projects. Being exempted from final examinations meant that I could focus on the class projects, like writing a FORTRAN program.

Time passed quickly and my father picked me up. We flew home to Maryland where I spent the next six weeks in bed. I missed out on commencement exercises, which made college seem incomplete. Worse, my lengthy illness left me fearful when I started graduate school in the fall that I would suffer a relapse. I never again pushed myself so hard as that year.

Food and Development

O ne of the formative events in my early career as an agricultural economist took place at the World Food Conference
in July 1976, held at the Stephen's Theater at Iowa State University, which I came back to attend with my father. The conference
followed concerns expressed in the 1972 *Club of Rome* report:

> *The intent of the project is to examine the complex
> of problems troubling men of all nations: poverty
> in the midst of plenty; degradation of the environ-
> ment; loss of faith in institutions; uncontrolled ur-
> ban spread; insecurity of employment; alienation
> of youth; rejections of traditional values; and infla-
> tion and other monetary and economic disruptions
> [which have] three characteristics in common: they
> occur to some degree in all societies; they contain
> technical, social, economic, and political elements;
> and, most important of all, they interact.*

The *Club of Rome* project, which followed the Organization of
Petroleum Export Countries (OPEC) oil embargo in 1972 and
world grain shortages in 1972–74, modeled the world economy
and predicted catastrophic resource constraints before the end of
the twentieth century. Because the best and the brightest minds
produced this report, it captured worldwide attention. The report forecasted that constraints on resources would lead to global starvation and, because of the primacy of the economic prob-

lem, the report called on world leaders to pay more attention to economics, particularly agricultural economics.

"*Ya gotta wanna,*" one speaker cautioned. "*Before you can avert starvation and save the world, you have to want to do it.*"

Before the end the conference, I took this challenge as God's call on my life.

Part of the report included a summary of the *Alliance for Progress* program for land reform, agricultural modernization, and economic development in Latin America, which began in the Kennedy Administration. Because the *Alliance for Progress* took as its model the experience with Operation Bootstrap in the 1940s and 1950s in Puerto Rico, who better to coordinate the program than Puerto Rican Governor Luis Muñoz Marín?

Puerto Rican economic development clearly interested me even before I knew anything about it.

CORNELL UNIVERSITY
The Divine Gift of Sledding

*A*fter living and taking meals in the dormitory at Iowa State, I decided to live off campus at Cornell University in Ithaca, New York. With independence and parsimony on my mind during a visit to campus in August 1976, I arranged to walk-through a cooperatively-organized house on Elmwood Avenue. It was located across the street from campus, housed twelve students, and advertised a basement apartment.

"The basement is unfinished and no one has ever lived here before," Tom, a Jewish physicist from New York City, told me as we walked down the steps.

I could see that for myself.

"We will rent it to you for fifty dollars a month, but you will need to fix it up."

"Great. Let's do this." I said handing him a check with a downpayment.

Having worked as a carpenter during the summers in college, I relished the challenge of converting the basement into an apartment.

During the week before classes, I hung a door on the stairs to the room, walled in the furnace, and wired several electrical outlets in the new wall. I also converted a small workroom into a study and organized the abandoned furniture into separate living room and bedroom spaces. The chief remaining challenges were a crumbling concrete floor and the absence of ceiling lights. Even with table lamps and ample furniture, the dark atmosphere made the basement an uninviting place to entertain guests and a depressing place to live.

My parsimonious living arrangements allowed me to save money for travel to Puerto Rico on my thesis project, but in the meantime I was isolated socially. That fall, Cornell had a record number of suicides and before Thanksgiving students demonstrated on campus demanding that the college be closed until the problem was addressed. I knew of half a dozen students and faculty who had attempted suicide, including one of my house-mates, an attractive pre-med student who overdosed herself unsuccessfully and ended up committed to a psyche unit in Syracuse. I drove up to visit her on a Saturday.

"How are you?" I asked.

"I met someone."

"Oh, who is that?"

"He's my doctor."

"Really? Tell me about him."

It turned out that this doctor had recently married so the chances that this relationship would have a happy ending were practically nil. But, rather than encourage her to remain patient with life, I lingered on her adulterous story and missed the intimate nature of her disclosure. Because of my inability to connect with the emotional side of her story, I could offer her little solace and felt useless as I drove back to Ithaca. She later returned to school only to drop out soon thereafter.

In the fall, I worked as a graduate assistant for the agricultural economics department, which entailed both research and teaching obligations. Short on cash, I stayed in Ithaca over the Christmas holidays to research the effects of milk taste on consumption. Cornell suspended most campus activities during the break and most of my friends traveled to visit family, which left me feeling desperately alone without much prospect of enjoying the holidays.

One Sunday after Christmas I woke up depressed and decided to go for a morning drive. Thinking about a park on the other side of town, I drove down the hill to Ithaca following an unfamiliar road, Cayuga Street, through the center of town where I discovered the First Presbyterian Church. Curious about this huge church with stained glass windows and an old fashioned steeple, I parked my car and entered through the rear door.

Once inside, I must have looked out of place, not having dressed for church and wandering through the building. My depressed state must have been written on my face because the music director, who was running down the hall, stopped, and introduced himself.

"Do you like to sing? Our choir could use another bass."

"Sure."

He then ushered me into the sanctuary to sing in a choir composed of local students who had gone away to college and returned home for the holidays to Ithaca. There I met Margaret who invited me to a sledding party that evening.

Sledding was great fun, something I desperately needed, and I began attending the church. When I later joined the church, the elders encouraged me to work with their high school kids.

That winter and into the spring, I worked with the high school youth group and joined a small college group. These activities got me off campus and relieved some of the isolation that I felt living off campus. Back in the co-op, I discovered that I was the only Christian who attended church and my housemates were mostly Jewish.

The Journey to Puerto Rico

*M*y father suggested that I follow up on my earlier interest in Puerto Rican agricultural development and make it the focus of my master's research, which made sense to me and delighted my Cornell adviser. By the end of my year of college Spanish, I made arrangements to travel to Puerto Rico in the summer of 1977.

Before my departure, my faculty adviser informed me that Cornell University had excluded me from the doctoral program because I failed to maintain a straight-A average in my classwork. I entered the graduate program in agricultural economics with the understanding that I had been admitted to the doctoral program so this decision came as a nasty surprise and left me without a clear career path as I prepared for my trip. The uncertainty and shame drove me out of my mind.

A close friend of mine at Cornell, Joachim, studied agricultural economics and dated a house-mate of mine. When he learned that I was interviewing for work, but wanted to continue my studies, he suggested that I apply for an exchange program with the University of Göttingen, located south of Hanover in Germany. Shortly before I left for Puerto Rico in the summer of 1977, Joachim finished his doctorate and returned to Germany.

I flew to Puerto Rico by way of Mexico City where I spent ten days with Eduardo, a Chilean friend who worked for the Inter-American Development Bank (IADB). While I hoped that Eduardo would share his IADB work experiences with me, he considered it more important to expose me to Mexican culture. During my time in Mexico City, we toured the Museo Nacional de Antropología which specialized in pre-Columbian artifacts, boated through a large park with canals in the center of the city called Chapultepec, and stopped to see an Aztex pyramid known as Pirámide del Sol.

Between the beggars, the small children working as street merchants, and the vast differences between rich and poor, Mexico City overwhelmed my sense of social justice. To see old men walking naked in the shadows of great cathedrals, startled and shamed me. Fearful that I would run out of money far from home, I bought little of anything, even from poor street vendors.

At one point, Eduardo bought a small trinket from kids after I refused to talk to them, which shamed me in my fear and financial insecurity. The same fear of an uncertain future that keeps us from offering charity in comfortable surroundings becomes obscenely perverse in the company of those absolutely destitute.

Eduardo's roommate, Cuauhtémoc, invited me to a *"fiesta de quince años"* in Veracruz, Mexico for Cuauhtémoc's cousin, who at fifteen celebrated her eligibility to marry. Her friends lined up to dance with me at the party, but at twenty-four such attention from fifteen-year old girls proved awkward.

When I objected to sleeping in a bed with three other guys after the party, the family put me up in a hotel. I woke up in the morning with a terrible hangover. Eduardo and Cuauhtémoc had left me the alone with no way to contact them, no Mexican currency, and no idea about what to do. They eventually came by and picked me up.

Later that evening, I found myself the guest of honor at a dinner party hosted by the young lady's parents who seemed anxious to arrange a wedding between me, the *"rich gringo"*, and their daughter. Like any typical fifteen-year old, she quickly tired of the absurd conversation and spent the evening watching television. In the end, Cuauhtémoc found me to be a great disappointment.

Cuauhtémoc may not have been the only one disappointed. After ten days of tacos for three meals a day, I complained about the food and looked forward to Puerto Rico. On my last day in Mexico City and tired of my complaining, Eduardo took me to a nice Mexican restaurant and ordered for the both of us, refusing to disclose the order.

"*Did you enjoy your dinner?*" He asked after we had eaten.

"*Of course—anything but tacos is fine with me.*"

"*You just ate cat!*"

I still do not know what we ate, but if he had said that I just eaten crow, I would have understood the sentiment.

Island Adventure

*M*y flight to Puerto Rico included a fueling stop in Guatemala and we arrived in San Juan late in the afternoon. I expected that someone from University of Puerto Rico in Rio Piedras would meet me at the airport only to find myself alone in the airport, the only white person in a large crowd of black people. While I knew from my studies that Puerto Rico had many people of African descent, I had never previously experienced racial isolation.

When I asked in my broken Spanish for directions to the bus station, I got blank stares at first.

"The bus stops out in front of the terminal and Rio Piedras is on the bus route," someone soon told me.

Rather than risk getting lost in the city on the bus, I took a taxi to the University of Puerto Rico and arrived as the evening sun set.

I walked confidently up to the front desk in the main dormitory with my suitcase, again presuming that the University of Puerto Rico expected me, and and inquired about a room. The student working the front desk had no idea what to say or what to do. As we were talking, another student hanging out by desk interrupted our conversation.

"I know a boarding house with a spare room on Calle Manilla," he said, sensing my desperation.

He proceeded to lead me to Calle Manila in the dark where he introduced me to Matilda, an old woman who spoke no English but had a bed in a double room to rent for thirty dollars a month. That night I took a shower and went to bed, wondering whether I had made some horrible mistake coming to Puerto Rico so obviously alone.

The next day I got to know Matilda, who was about eighty years old, rented rooms to both female and male students, but she shared her house with the boys and rented a small bungalow out back to the girls. Steel bars caged the entire house and we had no hot water or air conditioning. The room I shared had two beds, two desks, and two fans to keep one free of flies and lizards. Still, one sweated hopelessly all night.

Later that morning I visited a local bank where I deposited a large personal check from my bank in Ithaca that I learned would take thirty business days to clear. This left me with only two hundred dollars in traveler's checks to live on for my first month on the island.

That afternoon I walked around the University of Puerto

Rico and got directions to the Agricultural Experiment Station in Rio Piedras, where my adviser had written the director.

During my second full day in Puerto Rico, I walked out to the Experiment Station where the director introduced me to the economics staff and gave me a desk to work at. The men on the staff mostly ignored me, but Isabella and Flaca, both economists, took care of me. Isabella lived only a block away from me and gave me a ride to work each day and Flaca, a nickname meaning skinny girl, patiently explained things to me patiently all summer.

After a few days, Matilda introduced me to her son, who later took me out for dinner and drinks. He also introduced me to his beautiful teenage daughter, who unfortunately spoke no English at a time when I spoke little Spanish. She and I spent an evening on the porch trying to converse, but it was like a hound dog trying to talk with a duck.

Later in the summer, the entire office traveled to mountain areas of the island to conduct a rural survey. We walked long distances through banana plantations to visit isolated farm families. Often, they had no running water or indoor plumbing, but always managed to have a television set! Out on these isolated farms, we saw coffee bushes, mango, persimmon, lemon, lime, oranges, and many varieties of banana and plantain.

The mountain people who we met were always gracious and invited us into their homes. The women typically made instant coffee for us, which Flaca always turned down for fear of getting bad water, even though it was rude to refuse island hospitality. After refusing the coffee, at one point our hostess offered Flaca some fruit juice. Thinking that it had to be canned, Flaca accepted it only to watch the woman reach into her cupboard for a jar of Tang. Pobrecita! The expression on Flaca's face was priceless as she drank her Tang.

Walking around the mountains, we avoided the constant ninety-degree heat and suffocating humidity of Rio Piedras. The small towns we visited also had reasonably-priced hotel rooms with good restaurants that served fresh fish, grouper and red snapper at mucher cheaper prices than in the city.

When I wrote to Margaret back at my church in Ithaca about my experiences in Puerto Rico but failed to mention her sister's boyfriend, George, she sent him to look me up. George, whose family owned a bank, showed up at my place in a black limousine and invited me to his home in Bayamón, a few miles west of Rio Piedras. He considered my neighborhood too dangerous to even get out of the car and everywhere he went, he either brought an armed body guard or carried a pistol himself. George became a good friend, something that I sorely needed, and his friendship brought sunshine to my clouded days, as if my church in Ithaca was still looking out for me.

Late in the summer, I collected statistics for Puerto Rican agriculture and needed to run some statistical analyses. When I visited the computer center at the Experiment Station, they indicated that I needed permission from my director, which took most of the day to acquire. With permission in hand, I returned to the center to begin work and found that I needed a computer manual, available only in the university library. That evening I visited the library and found that the only manual on campus had been checked out. Late that evening I found myself camped out, waiting for a professor to finish his class so that I could borrow the manual.

In the end, I almost had a nervous breakdown because of the repeated delays. I never completed the statistical analysis that I set out to do. But I did learn the meaning of the word, mañana, and from that day forward, I carried an *"emergency book"* with me everywhere that I went. Instead of getting angry, I patiently read my book, as I do even today.

A couple weeks before leaving Puerto Rico, I began walking to a local church on Sundays. I enjoyed the services and realized that the Spanish Bible provided a great resource for language study. Because I knew my English Bible, I could understand the Spanish without looking up the words in a dictionary, which saved a lot of time. One of the first things that I did when I returned to Ithaca was to order a Spanish Bible from the American Bible Society.

Twenty-Fifth Anniversary

*B*y the first week in August in Puerto Rico, I had completed my work. I still lacked a thesis subject, but I had reams of statistical data that could be better analyzed at Cornell University than at the Agricultural Experiment Station in Rio Piedras. So I contemplated going home earlier than planned.

My parents had a twenty-fifth anniversary on September 13th, 1977 but because my siblings were still in school, they moved the celebration to late August at Central Reformed Church in Oskaloosa, Iowa, where they had been married, Although I had sent my regrets earlier, my early departure offered the opportunity for me to attend the celebration.

My uncle Hubert, who was actually my grandfather's cousin and a lifelong friend of my father, normally attended such family gatherings and lived north of Des Moines in Clarion, Iowa. Because he would be driving through Des Moines on his way to Oskaloosa, I wrote and asked him to pick me up at the Des Moines airport. This would allow us an hour and a half to catch up on our usual political discussions and make my attendance at my parent's anniversary a complete surprise. Hubert liked the idea and promised to pick me up.

When we arrived in Oskaloosa, Hubert parked on the

street south of the church and we walked down the steps into fellowship hall. By chance, my father walked up those same steps without taking notice of me, because I was supposed to be in Puerto Rico. However, close behind him came my mother who immediately burst into tears when she saw me.

So often in ministry, we hear about people suffering anniversaries, which mark the death of a loved one or some other tragedy. Equally important are the joyous anniversaries where we honor our loved ones and celebrate the blessings of this life.

Latin American Missions

*A*s I worked to complete my thesis after I returned from Puerto Rico in the fall of 1977, my anxiety grew. As the son of a well-known agricultural economist, I would live in my father's shadow the rest of my life if I failed to complete my doctorate. I therefore explored options that would allow me to improve my Spanish, continue in Latin American studies, and complete my doctorate. My uncle John, a pastor, suggested that I consider working in missions for the Reformed Church in America (RCA).

The RCA sought missionaries to work in Latin America. RCA was committed to alleviating world hunger and continued working in Latin America after most aid groups had moved to more politically attractive regions, such as Africa and the Middle East. I eagerly applied.

The interview involved a day trip to Princeton, New Jersey to take a psychological examination which included written tests, such as a Rorschach test, and discussions, which focused on a recreational scene that I was asked to draw. I drew a picture of a tennis match.

In going over the Rorschach test, the evaluator expressed surprised that I noticed an increasing use of color in the ink blots, as if no one had previously noticed. The picture of a tennis match also interested him because it pictured me with my best friend, also a candidate for ministry.

The interview that followed focused more on the mission than the psychological examination. The interviewer emphasized the relational component required for effective ministry, while I focused more on the technical requirements, having recently finished graduate work in agricultural development. When we discussed salary, I flinched because working full-time for the RCA I would earn less than the internship I had had the previous summer working for the federal government. If I had completed a seminary degree, he explained, the RCA could offer me a higher salary. Then, he informed me that the RCA required that missionaries commit to a ten-year assignment.

Ten years! I thought, as my heart sank.

I thought of entering missions for two or three years, but ten years seemed like an eternity. In my entire life, I had never planned more than five years in the future. When I should have thought about the good work that I could do for the Lord as a missionary, I thought, like a typical single-guy, twenty-six years old, about what woman would date a poor missionary planning to disappear for an entire decade to parts unknown? It never occurred to me that someone else might share my enthusiasm for missions or that I might meet someone interesting along the way.

It is no wonder that the interviewer passed over my examination results; the idea of a ten-year commitment freaked me out. I left the interview distraught over my school situation and the prospect of never enjoying a decent job and having a normal family life.

The Road to Germany

*A*t the end of the summer in 1977 when I returned from Puerto Rico, my housemate, Tom, picked me up from the Ithaca airport.

"Tom, thank you for taking time to pick me up. It is so good to be home again."

"Steve—I have some bad news. Your friend Joachim died in a motorcycle accident on the autobahn while you were gone."

As I mourned Joachim's death that fall, I took his advice and spent about a week completing the application for the Cornell-Göttengen exchange program. While studying abroad seemed exotic, it would offer sparkle to my resume and give me time to apply for another doctoral program without the stigma of a break in my studies.

Months passed as I wrote and defended my thesis. The U.S. Census Bureau took an interest in my thesis and invited me to lead a team tasked with undertaking the Census of Puerto Rican agriculture, starting in June 1978. However, before I could return to Washington D.C. to assume the position, I received an unexpected telephone call in the office.

"Woud you like to go to Germany?" A very German voice

asked.

"When do you need an answer?"

"Woud you want to go to Germany?"

I managed to persuade him to let me call him back in the morning. In the meantime, I called my father who advised me to talk to my supervisor at the Census Bureau so I called him.

"Take the fellowship; go to Germany!" he told me, after I explained about the fellowship that I had been offered.

So I accepted the fellowship. I later learned that six other applicants, all in the German studies program, refused the fellowship before they called me.

The idea of studying in Germany excited and scared me. The town of Göttingen appeared on no German map that I could find and the correspondence that I received from the university proved incomprehensible. My parents recruited a German friend from Lewinsville Presbyterian Church to tutor me in the language, but we spent too much time chatting and not enough time studying. Before I departed for Germany, I applied for a doctoral program at Michigan State University.

When I left for Germany, I took it on faith that once I arrived I could find the university. My flight with Icelandic Airlines flew to Luxembourg where the station-master directed me to the train to Göttingen, which required a day's travel. By the time I arrived in Göttingen, the youth hostel where I planned to spend the night had closed its doors and before I figured that out my taxi driver had left. Consequently, I found myself exhausted from the trip and wandering around the neighborhood looking for help.

I ran into a man attending a meeting in a nearby school. He deduced my problem from my broken German, but was obviously annoyed that I sought his help. Reluctantly he took me back to the hostel and started throwing pebbles at the director's window. Finally, the director let me in, helped me get settled into a bunk, and took me to join the other residents in their evening meal.

In the morning, the director moved me from a bunk bed in the dormitory to a private bedroom where a young man, who worked as a janitor in the hostel, came by to visit. We tried without success to communicate in German. But being Polish, not German, he spoke passable English.

"Do you know of a good university to study at in the United States? He asked.

After breakfast, I set out to find the international student office, where I learned that I had arrived a week late. University registration required that I visit a number of government offices and take a medical examination, as well as move into the dormitory. I also found the department of agricultural economics where they gave me an office and access to a hard-working secretary.

Evangelische Kirche

*L*ike typical students in those days, I traveled to Germany wearing a winter coat and carrying a backpack, which left little space for a full-size Bible so I brought a New Testament with Psalms. While I mostly studied the New Testament, I missed having a complete Bible and bought my first German Bible with a concordance. The German Bible that I had purchased from the American Bible Society back in the states excluded a concordance, which made it harder to work with. I loved my new Bible.

Not long after I arrived in Germany, I sought a church. From my dormitory on Rosenbachweg, I could walk or take the bus to a number of churches, but few had a more than only a few old widows and a pastor worshiping on Sundays. *Kirche Herberhausen*, a Lutheran church in a nearby village, posed an important exception.

In my first Sunday morning at *Kirche Herberhausen* I took the bus, I arrived more than an hour early and, because I found the church door locked, I stepped out for a cup of coffee at a local restaurant that was officially closed. But as I stood there, I noticed that people walking by me and around to the back of the building. So I walked around the back of the building myself and through the rear door, where I discovered a room full of men.

Apparently, the tradition of *frühschoppen* (morning pint) consisted of men tipping beers while the women attended church.

Students from Göttingen seminary and women packed *Kirche Herberhausen* every Sunday. Worshipers entered, picked up a hymnal from a shelf near the door and filled up the loft. The pastor entered through a door behind the pulpit, gave his sermon, and left again through the same door—never engaging the congregation in conversation or shaking anyone's hand. In Germany, clergy received a government salary and paid little attention to the morning offering, which seldom amounted to more than pocket change.

Following my experience at *Kirche Herberhausen,* when I arrived at Michigan State I began attending University Lutheran Church. The congregation elected me to serve on the worship committee and, after I volunteered to chair the committee, I also served on church council. While as a good Calvinist I later returned to the Presbyterian Church, I continued to appreciate the Lutheran liturgy and its role in fostering church unity in spite of divisive diversity.

To Postmodern and Back

*D*riving along the Berlin Wall in 1978, I saw crosses marking the places where someone had been shot to death escaping the *"workers' paradise"* in East Germany. Immediately I realized that America stood for human rights seldom respected elsewhere in the world, especially in the communist countries of Eastern Europe.

The contrast between the U.S. attitude toward human rights and that of the communists was stark. The inalienable rights mentioned in the Declaration of Independence in 1776 and enshrined in the U.S. Constitution had been modeled after the governance system of the Presbyterian Church and the Bible's teaching:

> *So God created man in his own image, in the image of God he created him; male and female he created them. (Gen 1:27)*

For Christians, human rights originate from our creation in the image of God which gives human life intrinsic value. This intrinsic value is, for example, the biblical reason for the death penalty. *"Whoever sheds the blood of man, by man shall his blood be shed, for God made man in his own image."* (Gen 9:6) Any other penalty cheapens the value of human life and impugns God's creative authority.

For communists, who follow Karl Marx's atheism, God does not exist and Christian teaching about human rights makes no sense because they recognize only the rights conferred by the state. Rights conferred by the state can be rescinded by the state; rights conferred by God supersede any particular state and last forever.

The crosses on the Berlin Wall therefore provided testimony as to why the source of human rights matters. Communists treated people fleeing from communist rule as enemies of the state who forfeited the rights conferred exclusively by the state. Having forfeited their rights, those fleeing who failed to escape were either being shot on the spot or sent to work camps, never to be heard from again.

The harsh reality of this observation was reinforced later as I drove with my parents on the autobahn through East Germany to Berlin. During lunch at a rest stop, I spoke with an East German family sitting at the next table over. They spoke to me and politely answered questions, but in speaking with me, they visibly shook with fear, something that I never experienced in West Germany.

Consequently, I returned from my year in Germany with

a new attitude about America and a profound skepticism of any leftist political movement that looks kindly on Marxism. As a young person I opposed the Vietnam War and identified with the anti-war movement. After Germany, I became sensitive to how the communists had infiltrated the anti-war movement. The same philosophies that earlier informed the Marxist atheism of Stalin and Mao Zedong, whose policies lead to the death of millions of their own citizens, now informed American liberals.

As my doctoral studies proceeded, I began to realize that the world had changed less fundamentally than I had assumed at a younger age. English was still English; mathematics was still mathematics; logic was still logic. I started to see traditional, Christian morality, especially concerning relationships and human sexuality, making more sense than the godless alternatives being promoted. As kids got hooked on drugs and children born out of wedlock had their futures destroyed, secular culture disdained morality and encouraged piecemeal solutions—if your spouse bores you, get a new one; if you get a social disease, take a pill. In the absence of God, the people perish (Job 8:13).

As I began to process my own experiences, I felt like the Apostle Paul describing his healing after the Road to Damascus experience—something like scales fell from my eyes (Acts 9:18) and what I saw in the coming years bothered me.

In my work as an economist, I started to notice how many people failed to do their homework in problem solving and research. While sloppy research has always been a problem, increasingly fraudulent or misleading research moved markets causing significant harm to millions of investors.

An early 1980s study of junk bond defaults, for example, by a professor at a reputable university claimed that junk bonds had been systematically undervalued, which led to massive purchases of junk bonds. Later reviews observed that the study only considered losses in the first two years after issuance, while the largest number of defaults occurred in years three and four. Before the financial crisis of the 1980s was over, the study's *"oversight"* cost investors billions of dollars in lost income and principal.

One can say that investors should do their homework, but whom do you trust to analyze complex data, if not reputable universities? And what happens when ordinary people entrust their money to financial advisers and mutual fund managers who depend on this research?

A new kind of subjectivism has emerged with postmodernism that disdains the idea of objective truth (God's truth) and made it harder to trust the many people—doctors, pilots, farmers, bankers, lawyers, carpenters, politicians—whom we depend on every day in our interconnected world. If people subordinate truth to their own subjective reality, they implicitly think to themselves: why can't the world revolve around me, my tribe, and my community?

Being subjectively defined, if words have no fixed meaning that we can all agree on, the potential for manipulation grows enormously. In the absence of trust investigating every decision imposes significant costs in terms of time and money on every transaction. I cringe every time another regulatory agency gets caught unable or unwilling to do the job that has been entrusted to them—unsafe food, unsafe autos, unsafe drugs—where does it end? In the end, there is no substitute for recognizing God's sovereignty over our lives and the stability that follows from it.

After Germany, I came to see postmodern thinking as having erected a new, metaphysical Tower of Babel where people cannot understand one another and I came to see the crosses on the Berlin Wall as a reminder of the one cross that really matters.

Summer Youth Group

*A*fter I returned from Germany in the summer of 1979, I met with the pastor of my parent's home church, Lewinsville Presbyterian Church (LPC) in McLean, Virginia. When he learned that I had youth group experience up at my church in Ithaca, New York, he encouraged me to organize a summer youth group at LPC. We conceived of the group as a college group open to high school students, but the college students took little interest. Meanwhile, the high school students loved the idea and it quickly morphed into a high school group with an occasional middle schooler thrown in.

Because I had little experience working with high school students, I leaned on the kids to come up with ideas for our weekly get-togethers. We tried Bible study; we tried group games, charades, and bowling outings; we organized a beach trip to Ocean City, Maryland—we had fun. What seemed to work best was to develop a theme for the week and invite speakers, often suggested by the pastor, with special expertise to lead the discussions.

One of my favorite group games was called, squirms, and involved role-playing difficult situations that kids might find themselves in. For example, what do you do if one night a friend calls and tells you:

> *Hey, I ran away from home and took the family car. Now, I am in Pennsylvania, 100 miles from home, and the car broke down. What do I do?*

What do you tell your friend? Obviously, such situations make you squirm, which is the reason for the name.

Squirms are more than a game for kids.

In the early 1980s, I learned that my pastor had been caught in an extramarital relationship with another man and had been dismissed by the church. Because he had been a mentor, went to see him and sought his counsel about my career. In the course of our conversation, I encouraged him to continue his pastoral work in the gay community. That was the last I saw of him. He later died of *"gay cancer,"* which is now called AIDS.

The summer youth group remained active during the summers and at Christmas break until many of the students finished college. As time passed, most of the kids found the cost of living too high in Northern Virginia and moved away, a phenomenon that I described as *"downward mobility."*

Unprepared

While I was at Cornell, I dated a French Canadian student named Claudette.

One weekend, Claudette and I traveled to her hometown to visit her mother. Claudette put me up with a friend of hers for the night and when she arrived to pick me up in the morning, she was visibly unkempt, shaken.

"My mother beat me up after I told her that I was dating an American," she told me.

Claudette went on to share that her mother had given birth to her out of wedlock at a young age and her untimely birth caused a scandal in the community. Her mother never married, became an alcoholic, and blamed Claudette for all of her troubles.

Claudette's disclosure exceeded my capacity to deal with it. I had no experience with physical abuse or alcoholism and neither the emotional nor the financial resources to offer her support. Sheltered by family and church, I never learned to deal with abuse, addiction, or a chronic illness and I withdrew emotionally. Over the next few months, our relationship disintegrated like a house built on a island sandbar (Luke 6:49) and we later broke up.

In my shame, I started reading about alcoholism, especially Howard Clinebell's *Understanding and Counseling the Alcoholic*, now considered a classic in counseling addicts. I learned to recognize the signs of alcoholism and the spiritual nature of the problem. Moreover, I learned to study brokenness before dealing with it—a lesson that served me well over the years.

At its heart, alcoholism poses a spiritual problem because, whenever we face a difficult problem or pain, we need to decide: will we turn to God in our hour of need or will we turn inward and immerse ourselves in the pain?

If we turn to God like Jesus did in the Garden of Gethsemane (Matt 26:36–46), then our faith offers strength and God promises to walk with us.

But, if we turn into our pain, then we look for ways to erase it, usually with our drugs of choice—food, liquor, sex, work, or narcotics. The addict has effectively substituted a drug for God and then treats it as a solution, not a problem in itself. This confusion over problems and solutions makes alcoholism impossible to treat until the alcoholic returns to the original decision and turns to God, which seldom happens until other alternatives are exhausted.

While I never became an alcoholic, alcoholism runs in

parts of my family, suggesting a genetic predisposition. My experience with Claudette and subsequent study of alcoholism alerted me to the problem of addiction.

Before I met Claudette, I frequently enjoyed drinking hard liquor. Afterwards, I gave up liquor and only occasionally drank beer and wine.

MICHIGAN STATE UNIVERSITY

Dance for Success

*A*t Iowa State and Cornell, I wore comfortable clothes—
plaid shirts, blue jeans, and army surplus jackets—and
grew a long beard and hair down to my shoulders. I sensed, however, that the faculty did not take me seriously because of my
appearance and it bothered me.

In preparing for my trip to Germany, I did not want to
stand out as an American. I trimmed my beard and bought a
brown leather flight jacket to match German fashions. My German assimilation plan worked. I also discovered that my intro-
spective proclivities and my Dutch family background dovetailed
better with German than American culture. For the first time in
my life, I felt like I belonged.

On my return from Germany in August 1979, I had only
a couple of weeks to prepare to start a doctoral program at Michigan State University.

*If dressing to fit in worked in Germany, why not at Mich-
igan State where I was fighting to resurrect my career?* I thought.

So I bought new clothes—a Tweed jacket, striped silk
ties, and button-down, white shirts—to upgrade my image. I also

continued to trim my hair and beard. I then packed a suitcase and flew to East Lansing, Michigan to move into Owen Hall, the graduate student dormitory.

At Michigan State, I began wearing a tie, white shirt, and tweed jacket to class where students and faculty alike treated me as smarter, wealthier, and older than I was. At one point during a field trip with a marketing class from the business school, the president of the company walked past my professor to talk with me. Upset, the professor who quickly introduced himself and corrected the mistake.

I enjoyed the increased attention at first, but I later noticed that I attracted *"friends"* who hung out with me primarily because of my perceived wealth. When they saw beyond the tweed jacket, they dropped me like a cold, wet newspaper in February.

Following the fashion advice of authors like John Molley, who wrote *Dress for Success*, works because the majority of people that you work with never see your work—they only see you. If you are well mannered and dress nice, they assume that you are also competent. It is a visual equivalent of telling people what they want to hear.

My German persona—short beard, tweed jacket, shirt

and tie—aided both a social and professional turnaround and had become my default setting by the time I graduated. The importance of appearances in my social and professional life, however, bothered me. I felt a bit like one of Jesus' white-washed tombs—pretty on the outside but full of dead bones, when real beauty proceeds from the inside out (Matt 23–26).

I yearned to develop real confidence to live out my faith and handle myself well in any social setting

Managing the International's Playbook

*I*n the dormitory at Michigan State, I joined Owen Hall's intramural soccer team in the fall of 1979 and started playing daily pickup games, indoors during the winter and outdoors during the warmer seasons. When the team manager graduated, I took over as team manager and renamed the team: The Internationals.

I recruited talented international players from the daily pickup games as manager, where I could observe them on the field. Many played varsity-level soccer in college. Some could dribble and head the ball in the air as long as they wanted while others could kick goals from mid-field. With such serious players, the mostly undergraduate, American intramural teams lacked the technical skills to compete with us.

Matched against other good, technical players, we showed our age. At one point, we practiced playing the Michigan State varsity team, whose players had good technical skills, trained hard, and were younger than us. In this match, we held our own for about twenty minutes. After that, they ran us into the ground, offering us a lesson in humility.

As manager, I could play anytime I wanted, but I seldom substituted myself into games when I had a full complement of players. In order to recruit good players, I promised to let them play an entire game, a promise that I worked hard to keep.

In my managerial role, I often played peacemaker, setting a positive tone to keep the team focused on the game, rather than player differences. One of our strongest competitors, the Iranian team, broke up over political differences and I recruited their goalie, a well-known Palestinian player. On our team, political differences let to conflict between Greek and Turkish players, but more typically our strong-willed players just got in each other's hair. I found it helpful to play a zonal defense, which gave everyone an equal opportunity to play, minimized conflict, and allowed us to adjust positions to match our opponents' strengths and to exploit their weaknesses.

We employed several strategies in competition. Most American teams fielded only one or two talented players, who, once identified, could be neutralized by assigning a defender to cover them. While this strategy meant partially abandoning a zonal defense, it worked extremely well in intramural competition. Another strategy came in recruiting a talented female player, who, should the men on the opposing team underestimate her abilities, would pivot quickly and score a goal, penalizing them for their prejudice.

With the breakup of the Iranian team, only the Pink Panthers remained a serious contender because their manager also recruited international students from the daily pickup games. The Internationals and Pink Panthers both typically beat other rivals and faced off against each other in the final match of the season.

In the final match in 1981, we dominated the game until the Pink Panthers targeted our star forward, who accused them of deliberately trying to injure him and walked off the field; the Pink Panthers then won the match and took the Gold Cup. The manager of the Pink Panthers had a reputation for dirty tricks and a white-hot temper, which worked to our disadvantage because the Internationals played a level-headed, clean, highly technical game. The loss of the Gold Cup because of a dirty trick left us bitter.

When we met the Pink Panthers again the following year, a grudge match ensued. We developed a strategy in the event that the Pink Panthers moved again to injure our players—when the referees looked the other way, our half-back planned to kick their hot-blooded manager in the shin.

As expected, as the Pink Panthers began to lose the game in the second half, they again became physical and our half-back executed the plan, kicking their manager in the shin. Kicked, the manager lost his temper, came out swinging, and got red-carded for his anger-management problem. Forced to play down a man, the Pink Panthers lost the match and the Internationals took the Gold Cup.

A Mexican friend, who played with the Pink Panthers, left the field in tears. When I tried to recruit him earlier to join The Internationals, he turned me down, saying: *"I want to play on the winning team!"*

While the Apostle Paul would have frowned on our strategy for winning the cup, he often wrote using sports analogies to describe the spiritual life, as in:

> *Do you not know that in a race all the runners run, but only one receives the prize? So run that you may obtain it. Every athlete exercises self-control in all things. They do it to receive a perishable wreath, but we an imperishable.* (1 Cor 9:24–25)

Paul wrote about sports, not because the Christian should enjoy testing, but because we cannot avoid it. We discipline ourselves to excel knowing that, otherwise, one day our weaknesses may bring us down.

After graduation, I played soccer for a couple seasons with an FBI team in Northern Virginia, but it proved to be a fool's errand. The FBI team never fully accepted me as a player and, because I could no longer train as hard as in graduate school, playing soccer resulted in frequent injuries. After spraining my ankle, I hung up my soccer shoes and focused on jogging.

The Killer Instinct

*I*n my first job as an professional economist, I interned with Western European Branch during the summer of 1978. Western European Branch was part of International Trade Division in the Economic Research Service of U. S. Department of Agriculture (USDA). Having lived in Puerto Rico and learned Spanish, they assigned me to research the agriculture of Spain.

In my literature review I learned that Spain ranked among the top importers of U.S. corn and soybeans and hosted important U.S. military bases in the Azores Islands. The United States supported Spanish entry into European Community (EC) to strengthen their economy, their political stability, and their commitment to the North Atlantic Treaty Organization (NATO). But Spanish entry into the EC also threatened lucrative U.S. grain exports, because the EC taxed grain imports to prop up local production, which made research on Spanish agriculture a priority.

I proposed to assemble a statistical bulletin on Spanish agriculture. Researchers loved statistical books because they saved them from the need to visit research libraries, such as the Library of Congress and the USDA library. Management enthusiastically approved my proposal, but the support staff almost rioted.

The staff disliked statistical bulletins because the tables required tedious manual preparation and proofing. As the project researcher, I spent the day looking up numbers in Spanish census books, translating the Spanish row and column headings into English, recording the numbers in pencil on lined paper, and tabulating row and column sums with a manual calculator. I then passed this table of figures to a secretary who typed it up on large sheets of *"camera copy"* with an IBM Selectric typewriter. The sheets were then photo-reduced to fit on eight-by-eleven inch pages.

Typing a statistical table without error challenged the best typists. Typists loved the IBM Selectric typewriter because errors found as one typed could be corrected by backspacing and using a special key to white over the offending letter or number. An error discovered after removing the camera copy from the typewriter could almost never use this method, because of problems in accurately aligning the rows and columns. Such errors needed to be painted over with a *"white out"* brush, which was messy and could only be done a limited number of times. If a typist made too many errors on a particular sheet, the entire table needed to be retyped. I went through about three secretaries before I found someone with the accuracy and persistence to type these tables.

Publishing a statistical bulletin demonstrated that I had the *"killer instinct"*—the ability to design, implement, and complete useful projects without supervision, and worked well with staff. This meant that I had the makings of a good researcher and would be invited back to work full-time.

Later in my career, I requested to work with interns, adopting the attitude of Barnabas. Barnabas introduced Paul (also called Saul) to the Apostles in Jerusalem (Acts 9:27) and later mentored him in Antioch (Acts 11:25–26). While I worked to introduce interns to the killer instinct, most staff spent little time with them and the typical intern spent the summer standing in front of the photocopy machine.

First Fruits

*A*fter I returned from year's study in Germany ın the summer of 1979, I traveled to Iowa to visit my grandparents and other family. My grandparents had rented the farm to a neighbor and moved into a house in Oskaloosa.

During this visit, Grandpa Frank and I drove out to the farm to take care of some chores.

"If you attend seminary, I will pay your expenses," he told me unexpectedly.

"I have been studying for a career in agricultural economics, but the girl that I am dating would rather just farm," I responded after a pause.

From the look he gave me it was clear that he thought I was nuts to consider farming a career option.

From Oskaloosa I drove to Clarion, Iowa to visit relatives who together farmed a section of land that my Uncle Hubert had purchased during the Great Depression. Hubert bought land when everyone else left agriculture because he felt strongly that families should stick together and that farming afforded the opportunity for children to grow up with roots that city kids lacked. Hubert mentored my father when he attended Iowa State University in the 1950s; then, he mentored me as I followed in my

196   *Called Along the Way*

father's footsteps. As a local Republican Party chairman, he took me to a political barbecue where he introduced me to the Lieutenant Governor Terry Branstad and to John Anderson, who was campaigning for president.

One of Hubert's daughters invited me to a dinner party, but after a few minutes I felt strangely isolated as I sat on the couch. After a point, I realized that the young woman sitting next to me was one of Hubert's granddaughters who had been a friend in college. I had not expected to see her because she lived in Minnesota and had also recently returned from studying a year abroad in Brazil. Talking with her, she also felt isolated from the family.

"Why aren't you folks visiting with us?" I asked the group.

"Why would you world travelers find our company interesting?" Someone responded.

"Of course, you folks are interesting. That's why we came to visit."

The conversation opened up at that point and became more lively—we even discussed the crops, weather, and politics! Hospitality always was a core value in the Hiemstra family.

Several years later in October 1996, my office sent me to an agricultural bankers' conference in Des Moines. Because my uncle, Dave, had recently been diagnosed with pancreatic cancer, after the conference I rented a car and drove to Cedar Rapids to see him. Dave graciously hosted me and we spent the day quietly putting puzzles together. Puzzles offer shy people the opportunity to hang out with one another with no pressure on anyone to make conversation.

What do you say to someone dear and close to death whom you will never see again? I thought, not comfortable with talking.

"I don't know that I am good enough to go to heaven," Dave told me as we took a break fro the puzzles.

Why is he asking me? I am an agricultural economist, not a pastor. Why didn't he ask John, his brother the pastor? I thought.

"God knows who you are; what you believe; and how you have lived. Your salvation is assured, even if life can be a bit confusing sometimes." I assured him, citing the Apostle Paul:

> *So to keep me from becoming conceited because of the surpassing greatness of the revelations, a thorn was given me in the flesh, a messenger of Satan to harass me, to keep me from becoming conceited. Three times I pleaded with the Lord about this, that it should leave me. But he said to me, My grace is sufficient for you, for my power is made perfect in weakness. (2 Cor 12:7–9)*

"If the Apostle Paul could suffer weakness and be saved, so can we." I argued.

My unpolished theology satisfied Dave, who remained ever gracious. Later, when I stood speechless at his door, he reached over and kissed me on the cheek goodbye, the only man who has ever kissed me.

Dave's question about salvation and my grandfather's offer to pay for seminary puzzled me for many years. I later learned that, as a young man, Grandpa Frank wanted to enter the ministry but he lacked his father's support and reluctantly took up farming.

Frank sometimes talked about the doctrine of the first fruits, summarized in scripture as:

> *Consecrate to me all the firstborn. Whatever is the first to open the womb among the people of Israel, both of man and of beast, is mine.* (Exod 13:2)

His oldest son, John, pursued a career as a minister in the Reformed Church in America, consistent with this doctrine. As the oldest grandchild, my grandfather looked for me to go into ministry and, in God's timing, I heard the call.

Iranian New Years

*M*y off-campus experience at Cornell convinced me to live on campus when I started at Michigan State in the fall of 1979. Outside of my department, on campus I met mostly internationals students. Many of these students were Iranian who avoided returning home after the Iranian Revolution by signing up for additional graduate studies.

Owen Hall pushed residents out of the dorm during the summer to make room for the temporary students which created a hardship for those of us without cars. While living off campus, every necessity of student life, from classes to buying groceries, required a lengthy hike. Consequently, one summer I arranged for an Iranian summer roommate, who owned a car.

My roommate and I reserved a room early in the spring of 1982 and, because we were only recently acquainted, he invited me to a *Noruz* party in Detroit, about eighty miles away from East Lansing.

Noruz is Iranian New Years and is always celebrated on March 21. Iranians celebrated *Noruz*, a nationalist tradition predating Islam, with traditional Iranian food, candies, and ceremonies. It was normally family affair, unlike New Year's celebrations here in the United States.

In the days before the party, everyone seemed to be giving me a hard time. Tired of having friends speak Farsi in front of me, I started studying Farsi. Between that and my passion for news events, especially foreign affairs, someone spread a rumor among the Iranians in Owen Hall that I worked for the Central Intelligence Agency (CIA) and a number of friends shunned me.

Meanwhile, my roommate teased me about looking for a woman interested in long term relationship. Any woman disinterested in me (and, by inference, a long term relationship), had to be someone whom he wanted to meet—or so it went.

When *Noruz* came, I wore a sport's jacket and tie, and joked with my roommate.

"Hey, now my gun won't be so obvious!"

Unacquainted with my dry humor, Parviz turned an ashen color and patted me down to see if I actually had a gun. He also wore a jacket without a tie, consistent with the Iranian, post-revolutionary fashion. Before and after the revolution, Iranians dressed more formally than Americans.

When we arrived in Detroit, I found that many of our friends from East Lansing had also driven an hour and a half to attend this celebration. Knowing people at Iranian social occasions was important because formal etiquette among Iranians required that common friends, especially female friends, make introductions. They serve as informal match-makers to aspiring couples.

Later in the evening, a smart and shapely young woman, modestly dressed in a black and white striped blouse with a black skirt and sporting a great big smile, walked in with her sister. I asked a friend of mine about this woman and her sister. She wandered off, made some inquiries.

"The two women you saw are Maryam and her sister, Azar," she reported. Then, she introduced us and diplomatically disappeared.

Maryam and I danced.

"What do you study?" she asked.

"I am working on my doctor's degree in agricultural economics at Michigan State. What about you?"

"I am working on a second degree in chemical engineering at Wayne State University," she replied, *"How come you know so many Iranians?"*

Because I am a CIA agent, I joked to myself.

"I live in the dormitory and manage a soccer team."

Time passed. I danced also with Azar.

"How about going to Greek Town after dinner?" my room-

mate suggested.

"I don't know. I need to study," Maryam responded.

"Come on; let's go; it will be fun," Azar urged.

Maryam finally gave in and the four of us spent the rest of the evening walking around Greek Town.

The following week, my roommate and I invited Maryam and Azar to East Lansing on a double date.

After being pared initially with Azar, I telephoned Maryam.

"Azar is too sweet for me; perhaps, you and I should go out."

"Is that right?"

After that conversation I traveled by bus to Detroit to see her.

Later in April, my younger cousin, Ruth, got married in New Jersey and threw a large wedding reception, where the Hiemstra cousins had a table to themselves along with other members of the family.

"Hey, Steves: when are you getting married?" My sister, Karen, asked.

"What self-respecting woman would date an old guy who doesn't have a job or a car?" I retorted.

Being the oldest cousin, marriage was a sensitive topic, given my age and the fact that I would graduate in a year or two.

By my age of twenty-seven, most of my American friends already had a car, a house, a couple kids, and, frequently, a second marriage. By contrast, many Iranian friends delayed marriage for financial reasons, which left them closer to my age. Furthermore, they lived disciplined lives, sincerely believed in God, and seldom divorced, being intensely loyal to their families. In spite of the Christian-Muslim divide, I often found more in common with Iranian than American friends.

My father later heard about my irritation at the wedding.

"I am going to help you buy a car," he offered in a side conversation.

After we returned to Virginia, my father helped me purchase a new Honda Civic.

After I returned to school, I found that my care quickly increased my circle of friends in Owen Hall and made it easier to participate in church activities. More importantly, after church on Sundays I could drive to Detroit to see Maryam.

Field Work

*I*n the fall of 1982, I traveled throughout the Midwest visiting cattle slaughtering and processing plants to interview managers and union officials for my dissertation research on labor relations, technological, and structural changes in U.S. beef processing and retailing. I started these interviews visiting plants in Eastern Market in Detroit, which gave me an excuse to stop by and visit Maryam.

Small, diversified plants in the Eastern Corn Belt closed and sold their machinery for lack of cattle while on the High Plains larger, specialized plants were being constructed next to massive cattle feedlots. The cattle in moved west because the Eastern Corn Belt had increasingly specialized in corn and soybean production for export, but the meat-cutters stayed behind and their formerly highly-paid, union jobs migrated to poorly-paid, immigrant labor. This vertical integration of two industries—cattle slaughter and beef processing—created production efficiencies through automation and introduction of vacuum-packaged beef, which had been frustrated by the unions since their introduction in the 1930s.

My interviews documented the human toll of this transition as managers and union officials eagerly told the stories of their lifelong employment ending and manufacturing plants being sold for scrap. Ironically, after interviewing so many laid-off workers, when I returned to campus in January 1983 I lost the funding for my own position.

With my grant at an end, I left Michigan State without finishing my dissertation. Because two-thirds of doctoral candidates never complete their degree because of an incomplete dissertation, when I left campus, no one expected me to finish. Students who failed to finish often listed their degree as *"all but dissertation;"* others quietly endured ridicule the rest of their careers. When I returned to Northern Virginia to move back in with my parents for the first time in about a decade, I was deeply shamed.

Classmates a year or two ahead of me interviewed for teaching positions, started work, and finished their dissertation research while working at their new jobs, as had been the custom. I myself interviewed successfully with the University of Hawaii, who found my master's research on Puerto Rican agriculture interesting, but they offered the position to a classmate of mine because he was closer to finishing his dissertation. A year later when I reached the same point in my program, Reagan administration funding cutbacks led the agricultural, land grant universities to curtail hiring altogether and, as time wore on, the field of agricultural economics entered a period of long-term decline that never reversed.

Hard times followed me home to Virginia. The Reagan administration announced arbitrary, back-to-back hiring freezes on federal agencies, including my old office in USDA that still wanted to hire me. Without a job or any prospect of a job, I lived in my parent's basement and worked days to type my dissertation on my father's manual typewriter. Once a week, I ventured outside the house to have lunch with our associate pastor, who considered me clinically depressed and a good prospect for his counseling business. I also occasionally interviewed for full-time positions in different USDA offices that hoped to hire once the hiring freeze lifted.

Although hard times lingered, I learned to prepare for the future during these quiet, transition periods.

In the beginning of a transition, we look backwards, lingering on the way things used to be, much as I hoped to enjoy the job prospects of my older classmates. In the middle we stop looking backwards, but still do not have a destination. This middle period is a creative time because we have a minimum of obligations to the past and to the future. College studies, dissertation writing, and hospital visits fall in this middle period, but so does most of our Christian journey. At the end of a transition, our new destination becomes obvious and we rush to meet it, much like I did when I later returned to work in USDA.

Ultimately, we will be judged on how we did with the open doors that we have been given (Rev 3:7–8). The most famous biblical transition is the departure of the Nation of Israel from Egypt (beginning) into the desert for forty years (middle) and then into the Promised Land (end). This difficult transition challenged the people of Israel, yet they learned to depend on God in the desert and so must we.

PART 3: LIFE TOGETHER

WASHINGTON AGGIE
Reconciling Trade Statistics

*I*n the last pay period of 1983, I started work at USDA where I joined the World Trade Branch (WTB) working with the supervisor for whom I had interned and who had recently been promoted to branch chief. I lived at home with my parents, worked nights and weekends on my dissertation, and traveled periodically school to confer with my faculty adviser. During these trips I always stopped in Detroit to see Maryam.

WTB developed and maintained databases of international agricultural trade statistics. After my branch chief suggested several projects, I chose a project to work with an old friend, whom the new administration had demoted from manager to senior economist.

The project involved reconciling United Nations bilateral (country to country) trade statistics with total trade (export and import) statistics published by the Food and Agricultural Organizations (FAO). Because these bilateral export destinations had to be retrieved manually from country trade statistics books, my friend spent the previous year reconciling statistics for only one commodity (wheat).

Comparing those import (buyer) and export (seller) estimates allowed us to identify both trans-shipments and missing data. Missing data might be trade with communist countries (e.g. Cuba) during the Cold War or trade in illicit goods (e.g. drugs). I checked with our computer staff to verify that these data resided within our computer system and, then, approached management with a proposal to automate the construction of these trade tables who gave me a few weeks to see what could be done. By the end of this project, I had a menu-driven, mainframe system for managing trade statistics, which the agency used for more than a decade.

USDA published our statistical method as a Foreign Agricultural Economics Report—*Methods of Reconciling World Trade Statistics*—which garnered invitations for our team to brief the FAO in Rome, Italy and the CIA, who took interest in our handling of these missing data.

Development of my data system led to half a dozen publications, my first promotion, and reassignment to Western European Branch, where I first interned. As my career advanced, I became passionate about my work and saw it as a divine calling, at least for a season. If all knowledge is God's knowledge then we cannot stray from God's work no matter what we do.

The Apostle Paul writes about this intimate connection

between our faith and our vocation:

> *Whatever you do, work heartily, as for the Lord and not for men, knowing that from the Lord you will receive the inheritance as your reward. You are serving the Lord Christ.* (Col 3:23–24)

My passion for the work also spilled over into my relationships. When Maryam and I married in November 1984, my friend and several other office managers attended our wedding.

Congressional Detail

*I*n the spring of 1984 I took a one-month detail with the Office of Technology Assessment (OTA) which followed technological adjustments in industry and found my dissertation research interesting. OTA rented office space near Eastern Market, a popular but sketchy neighborhood in Southeast Washington D.C. where walking, even during the day, required a touch of courage. But I loved the recognition that this assignment entailed for my dissertation and hoped that OTA would offer me a permanent position with a higher salary after my detail.

In discussions with my new supervisor, we decided that I would spend the first two weeks of my assignment interviewing around Washington D.C. and the second two weeks writing a short report for OTA. Because of the short turnaround time, I depended on the staff of the Joint Labor-Management Committee (JLMC) in Washington D.C. to introduce me to players in the meat industry and related unions.

One shortcoming of my field work came in finding and understanding union contracts outside of the United Food and Commercial Workers (UFCW), who represented most workers in the beef packing and retailing industries. New, highly efficient boxed beef processing plants constructed on the high plains typically opened with contracts with other unions, like the Teamsters or the National Maritime Union. These new contracts offered lower wages and fewer restrictions on management discretion that pressured the UFCW to match concessions. These concessions also made boxed (vacuum packed) beef highly competitive with traditional carcass beef.

The Teamsters, who normally represent truckers, played a key role in introducing boxed beef and restructuring the beef industry. When the JLMC told me that the Teamsters Union employed an economist, I asked for his contact information and arranged a meeting.

In the interview, the economist expressed interest in my research and I spoke for about fifteen minutes before I realized that he had been silent, other than to ask about my work. When I posed questions during the next fifteen minutes, he politely refused to answer them. Frustrated, I started to gather my things to leave. At this point, the economist waved me back over to my seat and proceeded to offer me a job with about a third increase in salary.

The job offer got my attention because it would have meant that Maryam and I could afford to get married and buy a house of our own, but the offer included a caveat.

"*This will be your permanent salary and you cannot request a raise later,*" he told me.

"*I need to think this over. When do you need a response?*" I asked as we finished off a steak dinner in the executive dining room.

He cautioned me to get back to him promptly because the Teamsters would start contract negotiations soon and he needed the help.

Wow. How could I turn down a big pay increase at a time when I really needed the money? I thought.

My conscience bothered me about working for a union with known ties to organized crime, but my usual mentors merely congratulated me on the raise.

By contrast, my grandfather—my spiritual mentor—cautioned me about this offer.

"*Why do you want to work for them bosses?*" Frank asked.

I knew in my own heart that my grandfather had it right and that I should refuse this proposal, but how could I turn down such a generous offer? After thinking it through, I resolved to ask for more money, figuring that greed would induce them to withdraw the offer.

When I approached the economist with my request, he

took it seriously, because he had cautioned me that this would be a permanent salary. However, my proposal shocked the Teamster president, who gave the economist a dirty look and waved off my request. About a year later a grand jury indicted this president in an effort to clean up the union, but he escaped conviction.

The temptation posed by the Teamster offer underscored my low salary working for USDA. In discussing my career with one manager, he offered me no hope for promotion.

"Kids don't care about having their own rooms," he said. Having been a kid myself, I knew that he lied.

Because Maryam needled me that my younger sister earned more money, I worked hard nights and weekends to finish my dissertation and rectify that situation.

From Trade into Finance

*I*n 1985 my former branch chief approached me about returning to Western Europe Branch to lead a a joint research project between USDA and an experiment station in Zaragoza, Spain. The project focused on researching feed manufacturing as Spain prepared to enter the European Community (EC) and had a tricky administrative goal of converting the project budget from an administrative travel fund into a research budget, as the project proposal required. To prevent budget tampering, I asked him to let me report directly to him and he agreed.

My branch chief had mentored me throughout my doctoral program and he liked that I followed my father into agricultural economics, as he wished his own kids had. His friendship made a huge difference in my career and I have often wondered why his assistant surprised me with a visit during my year in Germany. He and his wife were the only couple from my office that Maryam and I ever hosted in our home.

Broadly speaking, U.S. observers expected corn import demand in Spain to decline as Spain entered the EC, but the extent of the decline depended on the composition of Spanish feed rations and relative feed prices. Domestic Spanish barley substituted for U.S. imports in swine and cattle rations, but in broiler rations growers preferred corn. Because we had no studies of Spanish broiler rations to make this assessment, I proposed to make a trip to Spain to see if the Spanish team might be pursued to undertake a broiler study. The trip would also serve as a team-building opportunity for project participants.

The trip to Spain involved six weeks of travel in 1985 timed to coincide with a conference of the International Association of Agricultural Economics in Malaga, Spain (August 26–September 4, 1985). At the last minute, my branch chief got sick and sent me on alone. During this ten-day conference I spent time with classmates from Göttingen University, networked with agricultural economists from across the globe, and attended my first international conference as a young professional. After Malaga, I visited the embassy in Madrid to make a required courtesy call on the agricultural attachés, who also worked for USDA, and spent time in Zaragoza with my research counterpart, a friend and colleague from Cornell.

In Zaragoza I visited a number of Spanish feed manufacturing plants to learn about their feed rations, which showed energy (corn, barley, tapioca, etc.) and protein (soy meal, sunflower meal, etc.) substitutions, which proved helpful in a later study of Spanish import demand. Unfortunately, the Spanish team proved unable to complete a study of broiler feed rations.

After I returned from Spain, my branch chief informed me that he had been diagnosed with lymphoma.

"I know that I will die soon," he told me.

During his career in the military, he worked in a nuclear storage facility and received exposure to radiation that had already killed many of his co-workers. Being close to retirement, he tried to put in the six months that he needed to retire rather than leave government on disability, but never made it.

Even before he died, other managers competed to take over my project budget and I abandoned project leadership.

I requested reassignment to the European situation and outlook unit, but in my new assignment managers insisted that I continue research on Spain and the entire arrangement remained stressful, as I effectively reported to two managers.

As a country analyst working in situation and outlook, one of my responsibilities included making a quarterly export forecast for roughly forty commodities, which I automated with a Lotus spreadsheet macro program. The estimates from this program allowed me to grasp export trends quickly and, when combined with market news and diplomatic cables, could be used to make a defensible forecast. This forecast system excited outlook managers and I worked with the program coordinator to write up the procedure so that other country analysts could adopt it.

Late in 1986 senior management reorganized the agency with the objective of eliminating the international outlook program altogether. During the reorganization, positions throughout Economic Research Service (ERS) opened up for competitive bidding and I bid successfully for a transfer to the Rural Economy Division where I began a new career starting in Finance and Tax Branch.

Moving into finance proved challenging for me because I still grieved my branch chief's passing. With his encouragement, I had prepared for years to work in international affairs studying the languages, studying abroad in Puerto Rico and Germany, and developing an extensive network of professional contacts overseas. By contrast, I was new to finance, knew almost no one in the field, and was skeptical about the moral rectitude of the finance profession.

Nevertheless, I transferred into finance to avoid the administrative problems in my old office. During the next three years, I received three grade level promotions, something improbable where I had worked previously. The move to finance made it feasible to buy a house, to have kids, and to have Maryam stay at home to raise them. Looking back, I could not have afforded to support my family and attend seminary had I remained where I was and not gone through this stressful ordeal.

We are not promised a rose garden, but God promises to walk with us through good times and bad.

New Kind of Mentor

When I moved to the Finance and Tax Branch in 1986, carryover work kept me busy as I worked to earn my wings in finance.

Although I was new to finance, U.S. agriculture required substantial investments in land, resources, and infra-structure that left it sensitive to financial changes that all agricultural economists studied. While I never considered myself a derivatives expert, for example, in my first lecture as a teaching assistant at Cornell I explained how farmers could hedge their soybean crop through the use of the futures market. Thus, as an agricultural economist, I already knew more finance than the typical economist.

My interest in the financial sensitivity of agriculture led me into conflict with the Reagan Administration's policy of dismantling agricultural price supports. In the mid-1980s when interest and exchange rates fluctuated widely, the administration worked to remove policies insulating agriculture from that same volatility. This effort rendered the administration out of touch with the Republican base (most farmers voted Republican) and contradicted USDA's mission of supporting U.S. agriculture, or so I ranted.

After a point, I realized that my rant would make a good policy paper, even if it was out of step with the president's policies. Friends in management encouraged me to go ahead and write the paper, which was entitled: *Monetary Implications for GATT Agricultural Negotiations.* To avoid any clearance difficulties, I invited an administrative mentor to co-author the paper.

My move to Finance and Tax Branch proved critical to publishing this report because a finance paper would be reviewed within Rural Economy Division (RED), not International Economics Division where the Reagan supporters worked to implement trade policy changes. To avoid the appearance of excluding their input, I invited them to offer comments during the technical review but their concerns proved more political rather technical.

When on release of my report, the Reagan supporters moved to have it retracted from publication and the associate administrator scheduled a meeting to review their concerns. He refused, however, to retract the report which became so popular that the agency reprinted it twice. Later, I was invited to offer the keynote address at a national conference of the National Water Resources Association with six thousand in attendance the week before the 1988 presidential election.

When I presented this invitation to my new branch chief, he looked as if he might pass out—USDA refused to authorize any such presentations before an election! The invitation got kicked up to the Secretary of Agriculture, never to be heard from again.

Before we can offer salt and light to the world, we must first be comfortable living in tension with it. Behind the politics and office fights in Washington were real people whose livelihoods depended on our decisions—my own grandfather sold his farm and left agriculture during the farm financial crisis in 1984. It would be a years before I would find it easy to talk about this tension and develop the courage required to live with it.

Summer Doldrums

*I*n the office, having transitioned into the Finance and Tax Branch by the summer of 1987, my manager encouraged me to begin a year-long study of a legislative proposal to establish a new secondary market in agricultural mortgages. Long studies require patient, deliberate efforts to relieve the stress and it helps to have a backup study to work on when roadblocks arise. To deal with the stress of work, I began training in July for the Marine Corps Marathon scheduled for the first week of November.

When I began training, I had never met anyone who had run a marathon and had run only as much as ten miles. A twenty-six mile run was a big stretch both physically and men-tally. So with three months to train and knowing that I could run ten-minute miles until the cows come home, I set my goal for the marathon to run ten-minute miles.

In late July I went to my supervisor and proposed to alter my schedule so that I could train for two-hours over lunch. He liked the idea and helped me get a key to the building so that I could start work promptly at six in the morning.

Training over lunch turned out to be more fun than I had imagined. My New York Avenue office had a locker room in the basement where I suited up. I then ran down New York Avenue, past the Treasury Department, past the White House, and across the mall, where I could cross the 14th Street Bridge into Virginia, run along the Potomac River, and cross back at the Memorial Bridge. Military runners, starting at the Pentagon, referred to this river route as running the bridges and on hot days set up service tents to dispense cold water along the route. From the Lincoln Memorial, I could either head back across the mall to my office or, as I grew stronger, I could extend my run up the mall to Capitol Hill before returning to the office to shower, a run of about eight miles.

As the race approached in October, I approached my goal of running fifty miles each week and took longer runs on Saturdays to round out the week. One Saturday, as I ran my first twenty mile run, I started experiencing pain, like cramping throughout my body, which forced me to walk the last three miles and to give up training for the next two days. The unexpected nature of this pain freaked me out.

On Tuesday the pain still bothered me but I decided to try running again over the noon hour.

"Have you ever experienced full-body cramps while running?" I asked my friends in the locker room.

"Your problem sounds like dehydration. How much water

did you drink?" One friend asked.

"Dehydration? My coach in Junior High School told us that drinking water would lead to cramps."

From that day, I trained running from drinking fountain to drinking fountain along the Washington mall.

On race day, I drove to the Marine Corps Memorial near Route 110, which served both as the starting and finishing point. As I lined up, I joined the more than seven thousand runners at the starting line. Packed tight at the start that it took several minutes after the gun went off to begin the slow trot north up the route to the Key Bridge where we crossed over the Potomac into Georgetown. In Georgetown, spectators lined the streets and runners who had trained improperly started running out of breathe and throwing up. Among these runners along M Street was a former Secretary of Agriculture whom I saw bent over and heaving.

Those surviving the start breezed up to Capitol Hill chatting and waving at the television cameras along the route. I imagined Maryam at home cheering for me, but knew that she had probably slept in that morning. As we reached the East Potomac Park near Hain's Point, the smiles disappeared and runners began to hit the wall, the point where endurance becomes more challenging.

I reached a critical point as we crossed the Potomac River on the 14th Street Bridge when I reached up to wipe the sweat from my forehead only to find crystals of salt, which freaked me out.

"Forget about the salt crystals—They're normal at this point in the race. Let's finish this race." A fellow runner told me.

I labored to regain my composure, focus on the race, and to finish the final stretch on Route 110. I soon finished, had my photograph taken, and collected my medal. I finished in about four hours and fifteen minutes, which met my goal of running ten minute miles.

The following year I began training for the marathon in January and set a goal of running eight-minute miles. A grueling, hot summer followed with a record number of one hundred plus degree days in August. Still, I ran the bridges every day alongside of the U.S. Marines.

When the heat broke in September, I trained running eight miles per hour, which proved too fast. I over-trained, strained muscles, suffered fatigue, and caught a September flu, recovering too late to complete my training. Worse, running in the Washington haze in August gave me ozone burn, which left me with a raw cough for the next year.

I never ran another marathon. My knees gave out in 1989 which meant that I could only run with the greatest of pain. While I could endure the knee pain, I later developed *plantar fasciitis*, which involves inflammation of the bottom of the foot. The soles of my feet became so painful that after running I would sit for several hours at my desk with my shoes off and my feet resting on a plastic bag filled with ice. Although I stubbornly continued to run for several years, I finally had to give it up.

Running taught me about how our minds and bodies depend on one another. At one point, I found myself frequently depressed on Saturdays until I realized that I was not depressed, but physically exhausted from the week. If physical exhaustion leaves us susceptible to depression, then it stands to reason that maintaining our strength through exercise also strengthens us spiritually. As the Apostle Paul reminds us, our bodies are the temple of God (1 Cor 6:19).

Farmer Mac

*I*n 1986 while working at the Finance and Tax Branch, I began a study of the legislation that created the Federal Agricultural Mortgage Corporation, commonly known as Farmer Mac. As a new, secondary market for agricultural mortgages, Farmer Mac seemed exotic and largely incomprehensible to researchers focused on retail lending, which made it an ideal research topic.

Congress enacted Farmer Mac's authorizing legislation in 1987 as part of a broader bill to assist the Farm Credit System (FCS) in recovering from the farm financial crisis of the early 1980s. The FCS competed with small, agricultural bankers who resented the federal government bailing out their insolvent competitors. To gain banker support, Congress created Farmer Mac to offer bankers access to the bond market paralleling the FCS access through its funding corporation.

My initial research on Farmer Mac reviewed this legislation and compared it with the provisions authorizing similar businesses serving the housing market. Although I led the project, it took three of us about a year to complete the study. As subject-matter research in an agency focused on disciplinary research, the report got little attention. However, the farm press, the Farmer Mac board, and the board of directors at the Farm Credit Administration (FCA), which supervised Farmer Mac, took interest in the study.

In August 1989, I traveled to Baton Rouge, Louisiana, to attend a American Agricultural Economic Association conference, where I gave a paper on the agricultural land market and had lunch with the FCA Chairman to talk about Farmer Mac. I later interviewed for an economics position at FCA in their McLean, Virginia office near my home, which I quickly accepted.

The Friday of the week before my start date at FCA in September, my prospective supervisor called me on the telephone.

"Would you be willing to meeting me at J. Gilbert's Wood-Fired Steaks and Seafood after work?"

"No problem, but it would be no problem to swing by the office on the way home from work."

"No. Let's get together at Gilbert's."

Later, at Gilbert's he informed me that the FCA Chairman (whom I had lunch with in Baton Rouge) expressed concern that an agricultural economist had been selected for the position and he threatened my supervisor with a bad evaluation if he hired me.

"Did I really want to work at FCA?" He asked.

"Yes . . . Absolutely . . . I needed the promotion . . ."

The chairman expressed a political, not a personal, concern with my hiring. The bailout legislation in 1987, not only bailed out the FCS and established Farmer Mac, it converted FCA from the head office of the FCS into an independent federal regulator. Bankers considered agricultural economists too sympathetic to the FCS and unschooled in financial regulation. They preferred that FCA hire bank examination personal from the Office of the Comptroller of the Currency (OCC) in the U.S. Department of Treasury.

On Monday when I started work, after checking with my supervisor I left for Capital Hill to attend open hearings on Farmer Mac before the House Agriculture Committee. As the resident FCA expert on Farmer Mac, these hearings were a priority and helpful in understanding the legislative context of Farmer Mac supervision.

On Tuesday, the hearings continued and, as I prepared to leave from the office, I got an early morning visit from my second-level supervisor.

"What are your plans for today?" He asked.

"I plan to attend the Farmer Mac hearings."

"You cannot attend as an FCA observer, but you can take annual leave if you still want to go."

"That's interesting. How come?"

He then explained that the FCA Chairman called from a conference in San Francisco and made it clear that I should not attend the hearings.

The supervisor's matter-of-fact way of talking about what happened relieved my own anxiety and the hearings went on without me. I spent the rest of the day introducing myself to the staff and attending to bureaucratic issues.

Over the next weekend, to celebrate my promotion and to deal with the new stresses in my life, I bought a new studio upright piano and began playing hymns in the evening, as my mother had done for many years. For Maryam, the hymns remained her favorite connection to the Gospel. For the kids, the hymns signaled bedtime, when they were young, and, later on, time for friends to pack up and go home. For me, hymn-playing became a mini-worship service followed by prayer that has remained part of my bedtime routine ever since.

Living and Modeling Stress

*L*egislation enacted by Congress late in 1991 established a new Office of Secondary Market Oversight (OSMO) to supervise Farmer Mac, which reported to the Farm Credit Administration Board. Having written one of the few analyses of Farmer Mac while at USDA and worked on Farmer Mac supervision issues for a number of years, I applied to become the director of OSMO and senior managers granted me an interview.

The interview team consisted of a senior staff member and a board member appointed by the Clinton Administration. The board member was a flamboyant young man who wore a loose-fitting gold wrist-watch and carried himself very much like the President himself.

The interview itself lasted only a few minutes, after exchanging niceties and talking briefly about my work on Farmer Mac.

"What is most important to you?" The board member asked.

"I am a born-again Christian."

A wry smile came to his face and the interview was clearly over. He began to ridicule me with questions, suggesting that

I was more of a country bumpkin rather than a PhD economist. Friends later advised me that should have answered with some politically neutral answer like: *"I think that it is important to be honest, transparent, and treat people fairly."* But I had not anticipated this question and answered it honestly.

OSMO began with three staff members—a director, an analyst, and a secretary—and I was later detailed to OSMO to serve as the analyst. The legislation creating OSMO required that the office build a stress model for Farmer Mac. While I already built a balance sheet and income statement model in Excel to stress test Farmer Mac, the legislation suggested a more formal model that would be made publicly available.

In response, I proposed to convert my balance sheet and income statement model into a menu-driven, computer program. The new OSMO director liked this proposal and she sent me out for training in C and in Windows programming.

Bank Examiner

*I*n 1992, the Office of Financial Analysis (OFA) in the Farm Credit Administration's (FCA's) where I worked was reorganized and placed it under Office of Examination, where the objectives of the economics group shifted to risk analysis and examination support. As an agricultural economist, I had never been trained in examination so when examination training was offered to our group, I signed up for all that I could get and I spent about half my time over the next year attending this training.

Examiners audited Farm Credit System associations and banks annually to assure that they complied with FCA law, regulations, and policies. Because the business of the associations focused on making agricultural production and farm real estate loans, examiners spent much of their time reviewing loan files and repayment histories. A typical examination might last two to three weeks, depending on the chief examiner's off-site risk analysis. By contrast, FCA economists focused on policy analysis, market conditions, and financial performance, ignoring the business side of the associations.

Assigning us to support the examination function proved

interesting, but we now played by unfamiliar rules with unfamiliar staff, which made us look incompetent. Examination training helped alleviate our technical inadequacies, but when management assigned us to interior offices half the size of our previous offices, we knew that our administrative status had dropped and our jobs were at risk.

One morning in June, an unfamiliar examination manager walked into my office, introduced himself, and announced that my economics position had been eliminated. Because of my examination training, he offered me a position as an associate examiner in the McLean team at my existing salary, contingent on completing the examination certification program within two years.

Stress numbed me from head to toe. In coming to FCA, I thought that I had finally found my niche, working close to home in agricultural finance, but the nightmare went on and on. With two toddlers and Maryam six months pregnant, that morning I had no choice but to pursue an unchosen career in examination. I soon found myself traveling about eighty percent of the time with the Mclean Exam Team.

Because I had previously been consulting for the Office of Secondary Oversight (OSMO) when I was reassigned, the OSMO director arranged to get me a laptop available in the agency to continue my programming work on a part-time basis. Over the next couple months, I programmed the first version of a new Farmer Mac stress model while commuting long distances by van in rural Virginia and working as an examiner.

After several months of examination work in the McLean team, I applied for an economist position in the Office of the Comptroller of the Currency. The position involved data analysis and support for licensing analysts, who had typically been trained as certified national bank examiners. Ironically, my unchosen experience as an FCA examiner opened the door to this new career.

EARLY MARRIED LIFE

Courtship

*A*fter Maryam and I met at the *Noruz* party in March 1982, we got together a couple times, but after I bought a car in June, we started seeing each other Sunday afternoons after church. At first, I took her to restaurants around Detroit, such as in Greek Town or the Renaissance Center. Later, after she learned that I had run up my credit card treating her to dinner, she refused to eat anywhere other than Denny's. The bland food and the truck-stop atmosphere at Denny's irritated me, but I appreciated Maryam's concern about expenses and took it as a sign that she valued our relationship.

In August, my parents and I traveled to meetings of the American Agricultural Economics Association in Logan, Utah. On the way back, we stopped at Dinosaur National Park and visited the Denver Art Museum, where my father bought my mother a necklace. I bought Maryam a necklace with alternating gold-plated brass and black obsidian pieces strung together, the first jewelry that I had ever purchased. Maryam preferred real gold jewelry, but she always wore the necklace when we went out.

Traveling that fall to finish my field research meant that Maryam and I had little time together. In October, she traveled to East Lansing to attend one of my soccer games and to meet my friends in an evening gathering. In November after Thanksgiving, we celebrated her birthday and I gave Maryam, a pheasant-shaped vase filled with dried flowers, which still decorates our hall bathroom.

In December, I completed my field research and the financial support from my department came to an end. Early in 1983, I returned home to Virginia without my degree, without a job, and without much savings. I returned to Michigan State University periodically to meet with my doctoral committee and visited Detroit along the way to see Maryam, who still lived with her brother and sister.

During a visit in August 1983, I proposed marriage and she accepted, but buying a ring and setting a date would have to wait until I found work. A lot of details went unspoken that probably should have been discussed up front. Over the years, I have repeatedly reminded her that I cannot read minds, but in fact I also assumed that she knew more details about me than could reasonably be expected. But at that point in our lives we had stars in the eyes and details would have to wait.

Because the federal government froze hiring, I spent my days writing my dissertation at home—unemployed, destitute, and depressed. My father, who had been detailed to the White House during the Carter administration, returned during the Reagan administration to the Food and Nutrition Service in USDA, where he soon retired and joined the faculty of Purdue University in West Lafayette, Indiana. My parent's departure left my sister, Karen and I, to manage the house in Falls Church, Virginia for the next year before my parents rented it out.

At the beginning of the last pay period of December of 1983, my old office in the Economic Research Service hired me full-time. Having work, I rented a two-bedroom apartment in Shirlington, Virginia, close to my downtown office in Washington D.C.

Engagement, Wedding, and Honeymoon

*I*n early 1984, I invited Maryam to Virginia to discuss our future and arranged for her to stay with church friends. Working full-time made it hard for me to travel to Detroit for visits and we were at a cross-road in our relationship. We needed to formalize our engagement or go our separate ways.

"We need to set a date for our wedding." I began.

"How can we be engaged without an engagement ring?"

"Ring? I thought we were engaged."

"Of course, but no one gets engaged until they have a ring."

"Okay, but you know how serious I am about my faith. I cannot marry you if you do not go to church."

"Alright, I will attend church with you."

Maryam's promise to attend church was credible because her brother, Ghasem, and sister, Azar, routinely went to church and Maryam already believed in God and prayed. After our discussion, we visited Bailey, Banks, and Biddle in Tyson Corner shopping center and picked out engagement and wedding rings on credit. Still, no date was set for a wedding.

On a follow up visit, I took her to Kazan's Turkish restaurant in McLean, Virginia to discuss setting a date. Because

Ghasem and his fiancée, Vicky, planned to marry in Detroit in June and Maryam needed to sort out her immigration status, we agreed on a November wedding.

We planned a wedding at Lewinsville Presbyterian Church (LPC), where the pastor encouraged us to take pastoral counseling. While we sought advice on how to deal with the interfaith dialog between us, the counselor gave us a group presentation on financial management and communications, more appropriate for the younger couples in the group. Other than our poverty, Maryam and I had no problem with financial management and our only problems with communication surfaced only after children came into our lives.

We persisted in seeking advice on interfaith issues without success. The counselors within our network of friends felt unqualified to address the issue. Even Iranian-American couples whom we knew offered little help.

Both families supported our marriage plans, but no one on either side of the family expected our relationship to endure. We were an improbable pair and mostly on our own in dealing with the challenges that arose.

With the family scattered between Michigan, Indiana, and Virginia, and on a shoe-string budget, the wedding arrangements posed a logistical challenge. Maryam and I held the rehearsal dinner in the Evans Farm Inn in McLean, Virginia on Friday, November 23, which sat next to LPC, with the wedding to follow the next day.

My Uncle John organized the wedding service in cooperation with our pastor. Because our wedding took place only three years after the Iranian hostage crisis, I felt strongly that our marriage ran counter to the general prejudice against Iranians and might be considered a political statement. Uncle John merely saw two young people in love and preached his sermon accordingly.

We held our reception in fellowship hall, which was in the basement of the church. Friends from the youth group catered finger food. My best friend's mother organized a string ensemble that serenaded with traditional Iranian music.

Having given up our apartment to the Hajatpour family during the wedding, Maryam and I spent the night at a Marriott Hotel on Seminary Road next to Interstate 395 in Arlington, Virginia. After seeing everyone off the next day, we drove to Williamsburg, Virginia, where stayed in the Holiday Inn. We then spent the next couple days on our honeymoon as tourists at Colonial Williamsburg.

Outside of the old city, we visited the *Campus Restaurant*

in Greek Town, where I had worked in when I studied for a summer at the College of William and Mary. The owner, short and stubby and bald, met us at the door in his white bib apron with a butcher knife in hand.

"How are you and how is your wife?" I asked.

"She emptied the cash register and took off for West Virginia a couple years ago." He responded with a tear in his eye.

Maryam and I later ate lunch at the Colonial Inn, a fancy southern restaurant that I had always dreamed about as a student. More generally, however, she expressed little interest in Williamsburg or the amusement park at Bush Gardens, which we skipped entirely. By contrast, I enjoyed seeing the gunsmith's shop, smelling the bakery, and walking along the beach at Jamestown. The soot, the crumbs on the floor, and the dead fish on the beach didn't bother me at all.

On our last day we stopped by to see the old glass factory adjacent to the Jamestown settlement site on the outskirts of Williamsburg.

"Why didn't you bring me here two days ago?" Maryam told me.

As an engineer and chemist, the factory fascinated her and it proved to be the only part of our honeymoon that she ever talked about.

Wedding Gift

W hen Maryam and I were married in November 1984, I worked days at USDA and evenings on my dissertation. Having limited time and a limited budget, we lacked a television and did not need the distraction. Although I enjoyed watching the evening news, I preferred to maintain the ascetic lifestyle that I had in school. Maryam did not share my concern about television and her brother gave us one as a wedding gift.

While many Americans see Iranians through the eyes of Islamic asceticism, the role of Islam in Iranian culture changed dramatically with the ouster of the Shah of Iran, Mohammad Reza Pahlavi, on January 16, 1979 during the Iranian Revolution. Earlier in the 1960s, the Shah promoted land reform, social and economic change. By the time of the Revolution, Iran had developed a *"Hollywood culture,"* which reflected the strong influence of American entertainment on Iranian culture. For Iranians who grew up during in pre-revolutionary Iranian and later came to the United States to study, this Hollywood culture remains a strong influence and a symbol of resistance to the Islamic fundamentalism, both inside and outside Iran, especially for women.

Maryam always loved to watch television but for many years she was too busy studying for her teaching certificate and master's degree to pay much attention. After she finished her studies, the television would be constantly on, much like in the day room of psychiatric ward.

"*There is nothing on,*" she would complain.

"*That's why it has an off button. Who needs such mind-trash.*" I would respond.

"*You're so boring. When I die, I want to be buried with the television remote in my hand.*"

Much later, television interfered with the kid's bedtime routines. But, Maryam loved to stay up late watching television and insisted that the kids watch with her. As an early riser, I argued that the kids needed to go to bed before the adults and having them buzzed up on a show lengthened the process. Although I normally managed the bedtime routine when the kids remained young, this routine proved impossible to enforce when the kids reached middle school.

Wonder Woman

When Maryam and I were married, we lived in a two-bedroom apartment in Shirlington, Virginia, close to my office in Southwest Washington. Our families lent us money for the cars and donated furniture to help us get started. Once we settled ours debts, we begin saving for a place of our own. While I worked days for the USDA and I worked evenings on the dissertation, Maryam worked retail and looked for professional work in chemistry or engineering.

I started work at the USDA earning a wage meager relative to the cost of living in Northern Virginia. Our Shirlington apartment had solid construction with a stone exterior and hardwood floors, but the affordable rent came with a sketchy neighborhood between misbehaving neighbors, nearby drug sales, and an encroaching urban environment. When my elderly mother-in-law, who spoke no English, visited and suffered verbal abuse from a relative of the apartment owners, I complained but remained deeply ashamed that I could not afford a safer neighborhood.

Maryam looked for work in chemistry and chemical engineering, where she had earned dual bachelor's of science degrees, but defense contracting dominated engineering work in Northern Virginia and she lacked a green card. At one point, she interviewed with a company looking for a chemist outside of defense, but when I picked Maryam up, the interviewer looked visibly disturbed to see me, and Maryam received no follow up interview. While we applied for her green card, resentment against Iranians ran bitterly deep in the Reagan years, and we could not successfully navigate the byzantine process alone. She simply could not work as an engineer in in Northern Virginia.

For a long time, Maryam worked for a fashionable woman's chain, Thimbles, at Tyson Corner shopping center where no one asked about her immigration status. Maryam worked hard, routinely outselling the other sales staff, starring in store modeling shows, and helping out in stores across the region. With her bonuses, she accumulated a substantial wardrobe of suits and dresses bought at a deep discount.

During this period, we worked and saved and seldom rested. Maryam dropped me off in the office at six in the morning and drove to the mall where she hung out until the store opened at ten. Later, she picked me up and we had dinner together.

Early in our marriage, Maryam cooked mostly Iranian dishes, like *ghormeh sabzi,* and I baked fresh bread, both of which take a lot of time to prepare. Conflict in our household typically arose during dinner conversation.

Dinner conflict styles differed between the Hajatpoura and Hiemstra families. In the Hajatpour family, disagreements required a lot of drama to sort out while the Hiemstra family worked out disagreements more tactfully. Between us, disagreements initially favored the Hajatpour approach.

Typical fights focused, not on our relationship, but on unreasonable demands placed on us by other family members. It was annoying to have dinner interrupted by daily telephone calls or to have unwanted furniture dumped off, thinking we would want it because we were poor. And, exactly how many times could a particularly insensitive party be forgiven? The Apostle Peter, who recommended seven times, could not have been a Hajatpour or Hiemstra (Matt 18:21–22).

After dinner I worked on my dissertation until eight or nine in the evening, jogged for half an hour, and then studied until going the bed. When I returned to East Lansing, Michigan to defend my dissertation in May 1985, faculty and students alike expressed surprise that I was graduating and I discovered that most of the colleagues I had left behind had not yet finished their degrees. Most often, students who left campus never finished their dissertations because life off campus is too distracting.

With my dissertation behind me, we entered 1986 looking for a home of our own. We looked in vain for an affordable new home close to my office and family in McLean. We finally settled for a three-bedroom house on Shipley Court in Centreville, Virginia.

Maryam began substitute teaching in the public schools. Maryam could teach mathematics and chemistry classes and teachers from high schools across Fairfax County began requesting her for long-term, substituting assignments. What's more, she discovered that she enjoyed teaching, had a knack for maintaining discipline, and quickly bonded with troubled students, many of whom were also immigrants. Maryam studied for a teaching certificate and later earned a master's degree in education at George Mason University.

Dressed to kill with her fast-paced gait and the clomp-clomp-clomp of her pumps, Maryam set herself apart as a teacher, as much with her appearance as with her work ethic. Whether she worked with troubled teens, immigrants, or the de-motivated, kids responded to her and their test scores always exceeded the scores of other teachers' students. She worked long hours and refused to let her kids think of themselves as dumb. It was as if she were a one-woman Navy Seal Team fighting to keep the *Jihadis* from claiming one more hopeless recruit by introducing kids to mathematics and chemistry, and convincing them that they could do it. Early on I realized that I had married *Wonder Woman*, but her siblings called her *Ziba*, which means beautiful.

One afternoon in the mail, we received a flyer from Senator Paul Trible which described his legislative accomplishments and solicited feedback on issues of concern. I responded to his solicitation and described our problems with the Immigration and Naturalization Service (INS). Not long afterwards, we received a letter from Senator Trible inviting us to call his office about the INS problem. When we called, his office intervened on our behalf with the INS and Maryam soon had her green card.

By 1987, I felt confident enough to train for the Marine Corps Marathon, rationalizing to myself that with a new job in finance, I could not expect to be promoted and could take the time to train. But my supervisor promoted me anyway! I trained again in 1988 and received a second promotion! At this point, I could afford to pay family expenses without Maryam's salary and we began thinking about having children.

New Church Plant

*A*fter we married, Maryam and I continued worshiping Sundays at Lewinsville Presbyterian Church (LPC). The long commute became tedious, making participation in church activities during the week difficult. When we received a circular in the mail about a church being organized in Centreville, we decided to check it out.

On Sunday, January 18, 1987 it snowed making the commute to McLean unappealing so we decided to check out the new church. The circular directed us to Chantilly National Golf and Country Club on Braddock Road, about two miles from our home on Shipley Court. The sign in the club lobby directed us down a long, narrow hallway past the bar to a meeting room in the back. As we walked past the bar, patrons turned around in their stools and gave us a dirty look. While Maryam normally turned heads when she walked by others, I seldom garnered such attention. When we arrived in the back meeting room, forty to fifty people packed the meeting room.

Reverend Richard (Dick) G. Hutcheson, Jr., preached that morning. He was an experienced and stately speaker, a retired Navy chaplain who had risen to the rank of Admiral. I remember the elegant cadence of his voice and his eloquent rhetorical flourishes. After the service, Pastor Hutcheson recruited volunteers for several new church committees.

After the country club withdrew their support, the congregation met the following week in a drafty, neighborhood clubhouse in Little Rocky Run. Ironically, while churches have long been disparaged as being mere country clubs, Centreville Presbyterian Church began its corporate life being kicked out of one.

Vienna Presbyterian Church (VPC) drafted Pastor Hutcheson out of retirement to launch the mission, promising him that he could leave after six months, which he did. Dick had his heart set on writing a book, not on pastoring another church. After he left, the mission floundered without strong pastoral leadership. Within a few weeks of Hutcheson's departure, fewer than twenty people were attending Sunday morning worship.

Without pastoral leadership, lay leaders gradually filled the void. One of these was an energetic charismatic named Ben, who frequently opened worship services. Already that first Sunday in Little Rocky Run, Ben recruited me to join the pastoral nominating committee (PNC) while he focused on the steering committee. I later joined the steering committee and the choir.

The choir, which was the single largest group in the church, met in Mary's townhouse near Newton Patent Drive.

Mary and Jean were retirees and good friends who shared an interest in fine arts. Other choir members included Ken, Cathy, and Maryam, who accompanied me to practices but never sang. Sherry, who was short, thin, and energetic, directed the choir, selected our music, and accompanied on piano. We practiced hymns and choral music borrowed from other local churches and some Sundays we made up half the congregation.

This early steering committee worked less formally than a session. Few in the Centreville group had a Presbyterian background and two-thirds of the committee represented VPC or other churches in National Capital Presbytery (NCP). Important decisions affecting the mission were often made offsite—to this day I do not know who recruited our supply pastors.

The PNC shared this three-part division. Because VPC financed the Centreville mission, a quiet, VPC fundamentalist, Sam, chaired the committee. The Byzantine call process plus the committee political divisions made the PNC's work long and hard. After about eighteen months of reviewing personal information forms and interviewing selected candidates, the committee narrowed the list to three candidates, one for each division. NCP volunteers supported a local female pastor with church-planting experience; VPC volunteers supported a pastor from Indiana; and Centreville volunteers supported a stately pastor who reminded me of Pastor Hutcheson.

On my recommendation, the PNC proceeded to call each of these three candidates in the above order until one accepted the call. The NCP candidate refused the call because she did not receive unanimous support; the VPC candidate refused the call over the financial terms; the Centreville candidate, Horace Houston, responded wholeheartedly to the call and he accepted the position. News that the PNC had called a pastor gave hope to the long-suffering congregation. This announcement freed up PNC members, like myself, to devote time and energy to other mission projects.

Work for the mission exhausted me. As a member of both the steering committee and the PNC, I kept up at that point in my career because Maryam and I delayed having children. When I moved into finance, my career required more time and my burnout became more obvious.

The temporary lull in work in the Centreville mission quickly came to an end because Ben and Horace did not see eye-to-eye. Ben's wife volunteered to take over the group's finance, which signaled further conflict because the family would then control the two most important committees in the mission. Accordingly, I proposed that the steering committee divide finances between receipts and disbursements and I volunteered to take over disbursements as treasurer.

This attempted collusion must have also taken a toll on Horace who had an open dispute with Ben one February morning in 1989 in Sunday school. After the dispute, Ben and his wife walked out of church and never returned. Horace stayed until June, when after preaching on Psalm 103, he announced his departure on the first anniversary of his arrival and threw the mission into crisis. Sensing the threat, Pastor Peter James of VPC convinced NCP to accelerate the call process to replace Horace and quickly called a new pastor, J. Robin Bromhead, in the fall.

Once the church installed Pastor Rob, I sensed the need to give the new pastor breathing room. Exhausted, I divested myself of the church jobs that I held—the steering committee, the treasurer's job, writing the annual report, and chairing the chartering committee—and focused on singing in the choir. Maryam reinforced this withdrawal from leadership.

"Until the kids are three years old, please do not volunteer for any more church jobs," she told me.

My breather from leadership ultimately lasted more than a decade while I focused on my career.

Christine Arrives

*W*e had put off having children for close to five years after getting married because of the financial pressure and the need to settle into our relationship. Outside of the usual challenges facing newlyweds, we married later in life than most friends and we came from fundamentally different cultures. In spite of being Muslim, Maryam promised to attend church with me and mostly kept her promise, even if her level of commitment and mine differed.

In 1988, we happily announced our first pregnancy. As I was the oldest sibling and the first to consider children, our announcement received a lot of family and church attention. However, a week after our announcement, Maryam miscarried leading to disappointment and embarrassment. The following year Maryam got pregnant again without any mishaps.

When my brother, John and his fiancée, Julie Oweis, planned a wedding for November 25, 1989, Maryam, the flawless fashionista, scrambled to find a fashionable maternity dress for the wedding. We visited every maternity shop in Northern Virginia that we could find. Ultimately, we found a shop in Tyson's Galleria, commonly called Tyson's II Shopping Center, which carried a suitable dress. I remember less from the wedding than from the hunt for the dress.

In the morning of December 14, Maryam went into labor, but refused to accept the obvious. She insisted on dropping me off at work at the Farm Credit Administration and drove on to teach at Langley High School. Half an hour later, her water broke in front of her class and I got a call. My supervisor drove me to the high school, only a couple miles down the road, where I picked up Maryam and drove her to Fairfax Inova Hospital. She remained in labor until later that afternoon when our firstborn, Christine Nousheen, arrived without a hitch.

Two weeks later, on a snowy day after Christmas in the Alexandria Courthouse Maryam took the oath of citizenship with Christine in her arms.

WAKE UP CALL

Breech Birth

*A*fter Christine arrived, Maryam refused to leave her alone with anyone. On rare occasions, I might watch her, but almost no one else. As she drew closer to delivering our second child, Maryam's attachment to her firstborn became a concern.

The night before the new baby arrived, Maryam had trouble sleeping. She went into irregular labor early in the morning, but her labor did not move towards regular contractions every ten minutes, as parents are told to expect. We had not taken a child-birth class and did not know how to respond. After having labor pains all night, by five o'clock in the morning I became concerned and we debated calling my sister-in-law, Julie, to watch Christine, but Maryam refused to call. By five thirty, I called Julie.

Julie came over right away. Maryam and I called ahead to Inova Fairfax Hospital and drove there. On arrival, we checked into the natal unit and we settled in for a long wait, expecting a lengthy delivery as with Christine. However, the doctors examined Maryam briefly, announced that she needed an emergency Cesarean delivery, and whisked us immediately into the delivery room. The delivery went fine and Marjolijn Narsis was born a beautiful baby girl, but Maryam had to stay longer in the hospital than planned.

Marjolijn is the name of the daughter of Dutch friends, who rented Maryam a room before we married. Narsis is the name of an Iranian flower related to the daffodil.

When Christine and I arrived at the hospital the next day to visit, Christine held onto me rather than running immediately to her mother. Maryam was not happy!

In the following months, the family division of labor changed dramatically. Maryam could manage one child by herself, but having two required teamwork. A single child gets a lot of attention that cannot be sustained with two, because one of them always moves around or needs something. When Christine arrived, I bought a new 35 mm, single lens reflect camera and filmed her every move, but when Marjolijn arrived, we seldom had time to photograph.

Adding to our adjustments, Marjolijn experienced more colic than her sister, which left us tired all the time. No one wants a crying baby around. I remember being told undiplomatically one Sunday morning to move to the back of the church, because Christine was making too much noise. Unlike in the 1950s, Churches today mostly lack a cry room and churches expect parents either to disappear during worship or to delegate care to someone else, which we never did.

Late One Night

*T*he day Stephen Reza arrived, August 19, 1992, my office had scheduled me to give a nationwide video presentation to examiners across the Farm Credit Administration (FCA). Because I needed to show progress in my new assignment, the pressure to do well in this presentation was enormous. Maryam knew my dilemma that day so I drove her to the Inova Fairfax hospital, got her checked in, and kissed her goodbye to leave for my presentation. My office lay only about three miles down the road from the hospital.

On learning about my situation, my supervisors expedited my presentation and I returned promptly to the hospital. As a dutiful wife, Maryam, waited for me and, when I arrived, the nurses wheeled Maryam into the delivery room with me close behind her.

Stephen Reza arrived by natural birth without mishap and, to my horror, began urinating in the doctor's face. The doctor, who had delivered all three of our kids, took off his glasses, wiped off his face, and continued his inspection of the placenta and umbilical cord.

"What are you looking for?" I asked after a few minutes.

"The placenta and the umbilical cord could provide insights into otherwise hidden birth defects."

"Oh, that's interesting."

I thought nothing further about it.

The days went by quickly. Having been assigned to the McLean Exam Team that fall, I traveled from Monday morning to Thursday evening assisting with association examinations in rural Virginia. Because of my frequent travel, Maryam followed the Iranian custom of keeping Reza's crib in our bedroom, which made late night feedings easier. Then, one Friday evening in October, Reza went into convulsions. We woke up and called 911. Our ten-week old infant needed help.

The emergency medical team (EMT) arrived promptly and took Reza's vital signs. Nothing seemed out of the ordinary, but Maryam insisted that the EMTs transport him to Fair Oaks Hospital. At the hospital, the doctor ordered lab work which showed that the electrolytes in his blood were irregular without an obvious explanation.

Early Saturday morning an ambulance transported Reza to the pediatric intensive care unit at Inova Fairfax Hospital where he stayed until Sunday afternoon. At that point, the attending physician noticed Reza's empty urine bag and ordered a sonogram which showed that he had only one kidney and the kidney duct had folded over on itself. Reza needed emergency surgery to restore normal urination. Reza and Maryam were transported by ambulance to Georgetown University Hospital where the doctors scheduled surgery for late Sunday night.

Sunday evening Maryam and I lacked sleep and the stress left us nearly hysterical. At one point I found myself alone with Reza in his hospital room where I only heard the sound of his labored breathing. On my knees and beside myself with grief, I bargained with God.

"Lord, do not take him; take me," I prayed.

Later that night, Pastor Rob stopped by the hospital to offer comfort as we waited for the surgeons to complete their work. Because of Reza's tiny size and age, the surgeons opted that night to forgo corrective surgery and inserted a catheter into his kidney duct to drain the urine. For the next three months, he wore a urine bag.

After surgery, Reza screamed all night. Because of the problems of estimating the correct drug dosage for a young child, standard medical practice stipulates that infants receive no pain medication. Three months later in January, we came back to have the catheter removed and the doctors performed corrective surgery, again without anesthesia. Afterwards, we again watched helplessly while Reza screamed. Screaming: I remember hours of screaming.

Monday morning I drove to an association examination in Roanoke, Virginia. When my office learned about my son's surgery, they called me back to the McLean office for a period of weeks and graciously reassigned me to a research project on lending limits, to keep me closer to home. Traumatized by the events, I never properly thanked my supervisors for their concern in offering me this assignment, which had a lasting, positive impact on my career.

Painful as these events were, God intervened to save my son's life. Had he not slept in our room, he might have died quietly in the night as another case of crib death. Had he been born even a few years earlier, he would not have survived for lack of effective diagnostics and treatments. Had he not suffered so dramatically, I may never been aware of God's call on my life.

Land of BOS

*I*n early January 1993, I applied for an economist position in the Office of the Comptroller of the Currency (OCC) that would not require the travel of examination work. With my son, Reza, requiring follow-up surgery, I needed to be close to home. I had a rough idea about the job, but they needed a financial economist and I needed to get back into economics so a minimum of questions were asked. When OCC called about an interview, I thought that I had died and gone to heaven.

The interview went quickly because few economists had both the computer and examination skills that they sought. I met with my supervisor and my second level supervisor, who took me to lunch and offered me the position. The position involved financial reporting based on data from a network database of licensing transactions, which required queries in the structured query language and the ability to read a data schema. A network database involves data records more complex than more familiar, relational databases.

The interview excluded visits with staff, which should have been a red flag. A typical USDA interview, for example, might include visits with the hiring committee, managers, and each member of the staff, plus a presentation to the entire department. The need for teamwork motivated intense vetting of prospective hires. However, like other regulators, OCC retained a hierarchical management structure, where team work got more lip service than practice. I never enjoyed the intense vetting, but the abbreviated OCC interview caught me off guard. My eagerness to get back into economics blindsided me to the challenges that this new position presented.

My new office, Bank Organization and Structure (BOS), oversaw applications for organizational changes, like licensing new bank charters, conversions from state to national charter, mergers, failures, and opening of new automated teller machines, which required OCC approval. Banks generally take deposits and make loans, while national banks must additionally include either national bank or national association in their official name.

When I started work later in January, the office seemed congenial because both my supervisor and his boss, both economists, sought my opinion in staff meetings. But a copacetic exterior covered up seething staff resentment. My supervisor had brow-beat the staff for years complaining about their lack of analytical skills. When he hired me to bring those skills to the group, their silent resentment shifted to me and I found myself *persona non grata* as a new employee.

Had I been more aware of people's feelings and sensitive to them, I might have saved myself much grief at this point. My office problems became even more obvious when my old supervisor invited the entire office to a dinner party at his home, which Maryam and I attended together. The staff shunned us both the entire evening. Maryam left the party distraught because of the obvious threat to our livelihood.

Ocean Breakers

*I*n the summer of 1993 Maryam discovered a lump in her breast. When the doctors diagnosed it as breast cancer, we found ourselves bombarded with highly technical medical information that we could scarcely evaluate.

Shortly after the diagnosis, Maryam's mother came from Iran to live with us and help us out. The kids called her, Mama Bozorg, which means grandmother in Farsi. Mama Bozorg often watched the kids while Maryam and I went to doctor appointments.

Throughout this period while Maryam feared that she would die of cancer and leave three toddlers without a mother, I questioned the advice we received from the doctors. Breast cancer is insidious. Maryam's cancer started out as a small lump the size of an eraser on the end of a pencil without obvious symptoms. Her mammogram revealed no lump and her doctors missed it; Maryam found the lump in a self-exam. So before outwardly anything seemed out of the ordinary, my young, beautiful wife underwent physical exams by numerous male doctors, often in front of me, and we contemplated alternative disfiguring procedures. It terrified her; it angered me. I felt violated—facing similar circumstances, friends of ours divorced. Robbed of our youth, we never had more children, much as we wanted them.

Desperate to understand the advice given by the medical staff, I stumbled on the National Cancer Institutes' website. The website listed recommendations for the standards of care for each type and stage of cancer known as the physicians data query (PDQ). The PDQ confirmed that Maryam's doctors had given us state of the art advice for her treatment, which reduced our anxiety greatly. Consequently, Maryam had a lumpectomy, localized radiation, and a five-year regime of tamoxifen, consistent with the PDQ.

Meanwhile, I hunkered down in my work and tried to stay employed at the Office of the Comptroller of the Currency. No work; no medical plan. Melt downs and pity parties would have to wait.

Fearful that I might lose my government job to another layoff, I spent nights and weekends teaching myself new computer programming techniques, such as C++, which facilitated more robust computer code designs and implementations. Fascinated with C++, I worked too much and could not be fully present at home at a time while we still had three small children.

With my parents living in West Lafayette, Indiana and my siblings located in different places, family get-togethers for holidays required coordination and flexibility. As the first in our generation to have kids, we often found ourselves coping with the kids without much assistance. At one point my sister, Diane, invited us to Baltimore Harbor to take a day cruise on her new boat. It sounded like great fun to me, but unable to swim and afraid that a child would go overboard, Maryam retreated to the hotel room alone with the kids while I took the cruise with everyone else.

Adding breast cancer treatments to our already complicated situation stretched us both physically and emotionally. I attended important doctor visits, but more typically I got kid duty while Maryam attended routine appointments alone. Fortunately, Maryam diligently kept her appointments and took her medications, as instructed, but she often felt alone in coping with our medical crises. She ended up wondering whether my family really accepted her while they admired her strength and self-sufficiency.

While we expected the medical problems associated with breast cancer to be immense, we did not anticipate the emotional and psychological effects that accompanied the disease. People generally support you until they reach their emotional threshold and then they pull back. Patients with chronic conditions get little emotional support and often struggle with depression. Maryam's depression continued years after her medical treatments ended and the doctors declared her to be cancer free.

We tried to cope with the depression by taking evening walks together and by getting out of the house more often, which helped a lot. But, as a stay-at-home mom, Maryam felt deeply shamed by other professional women, who constantly asked why she did not seek alternative childcare arrangements.

"I am a chemist and a chemical engineer, but I feel it is important to be at home with kids while they are young," she repeated when women would ask.

Consequently, it was not until the kids became established in school and Maryam returned to work as a teacher that she finally regained her self-esteem and overcame her depression.

Transition into the Economics Department

*T*he emotions associated with breast cancer pillage both husband and wife, but public sympathy and care focus almost exclusively on the wife. Even then, most people close to you offer sympathy and assistance for a few weeks, but after that, its gets lonely. I never missed a day of work in the office during this period, but when I had a bad day, my boss threatened to fire me.

When I started working as an economist at the Office of the Comptroller of the Currency (OCC), I had an unexpected ally. When President Bill Clinton appointed Eugene Ludwig as Comptroller of the Currency, Gene distinguished himself as a computer-literate attorney who took an interest in economic analysis and took notes on a laptop at meetings. This created a big stir in an agency that prided itself on conducting bank examinations with nothing other than a pad of paper and a box of legal documents.

One morning I helped a man with a brief case and a laptop to get on the elevator. Seeing the laptop, I recognized immediately who he was and pushed the button to the top floor. Then, I introduced myself to the new Comptroller of the Currency.

As time wore on, Gene re-organized the entire agency, insisted on briefings by the economics staff, and automated the examination process. Not only did I meet him on my first day on the job, I assisted him with each of these initiatives during his time at OCC.

After the Comptroller of the Currency himself, I had the distinction of being the second one in an agency of three thousand employees to request and receive a 486 desktop computer. When the computer arrived, the computer support staff deleted Windows and reinstalled MS DOS following their standard operating procedures. After the computer support staff refused my request for Windows, I loaded personal copies of Windows and Microsoft Office onto my office computer. When I requested additional computer memory required to run Windows, they dropped the memory cards on my desk and walked off.

Over the coming years, my computer skills opened many doors. When Gene tasked my second-level supervisor with organizing a re-organization of the OCC from top to bottom, I volunteered to assist with the re-organization and quickly began process-mapping business functions across OCC. Over the next several months, I drew roughly one hundred and fifty process maps covering every business activity deemed important and worked closely with OCC's rising stars, who later formed Gene's new senior management team.

Because of my experiences and connections, a manager in the economics department arranged a transfer into his group to put my computer-programming skills to design and program financial models. As time passed, I increasingly became known as a financial engineer.

Troika

O ur girls arrived sixteen months apart which meant that they were close and competitive. When Stephen Reza arrived sixteen months after Marjolijn, the pattern continued. More than siblings, as our kids grew to be inseparable, best friends.

Maryam taught our kids to speak Farsi which made it possible for them to have private conversations out in front of most anyone, including dad. Maryam, who insisted that the kids call her Maryam rather than mom or mother, leaned into the development of this private world and encouraged a skeptical view of anyone outside it. At first, I enjoyed the family intimacy, but over time I realized that this tribal closeness fostered co-dependencies within the family and often hindered healthy relationships with others.

After the youth group at Centreville Presbyterian Church grew large enough to divide into a middle school and high school groups, group leaders insisted that Christine and Narsis needed to attend the senior high school group and Reza stay with the middles school group. The three of them complained and I visited with group leaders, but they refused any accommodation to my kids' desire to stay together. At that point, the kids rebelled and refused to attend any youth groups. This decision left my children with no meaningful attachment to the church, a situation never reversed.

This dilemma cut to the core of who I was. My close-knit family and my community of faith conflicted and I could not reconcile them. The dream that I had held since I was a child of an integrated Christian family life—a new kaffietijd, a new Sabbath—remained out of reach because I lacked the faith and the skills to foster it.

The Bank Calculator

*M*y transfer in 1995 to the economics department initiated a period of intense learning, productivity, and networking. In this new assignment, I migrated a custom econometric program from UNIX over to Microsoft Windows and made it accessible to researchers lacking FORTRAN programming skills. The program cut the time required to estimate a model from weeks to a couple hours and allowed my colleagues to complete a number of journal-quality research papers on risk analysis over the next couple years.

In the course of this work, I became acquainted with a mathematician at American University, who developed the FORTRAN program years earlier in cooperation with a Federal Reserve Board colleague. After hours during 1996 and 1997, we collaborated to develop an assembly language implementation of a matrix class for interval mathematics, designed to accelerate computations for the human genome project. As part of my validation work on this matrix class, I developed a small calculator program to automate the computations.

My work group, which later became known as Global Banking and Financial Analysis (GBFA), developed a relational database in SAS of bank financial and supervisory data, which simplified quarterly oversight of bank financial condition. A study of liquidity risk, which management periodically requested, proved to be the breakout project using these data. The first time management requested a liquidity study, we undertook a lengthy literature review and followed up with an econometric study of liquidity risk, which proved inaccessible to most staff members. The second time management requested a study, I proposed a brief study of the examiner liquidity ratings given to each and every national bank. With the new data system, this study was easily completed and found an audience. Management loved it and we found ourselves routinely fielding questions about bank financial condition.

In our research work on bank risk taking, regulators often followed contractual risks (credit and interest rate risk) with great interest and only occasionally examined threats to the firms' survival (liquidity and failure risk), which I referred to as whole bank risk. As our work team began to focus on threats to bank survival, we became known as the whole bank risk team.

Because my work on bank risk taking, I understand the *Parable of the Talents* (Matt 25:14–29) for the first time. In the parable, we see a picture of several servants asked to invest money for their master, who was leaving on a trip. Servants who eagerly invested their money and took a positive view of their master were rewarded handsomely; the servant who hid the money and remained fearful of the master was reprimanded and punished. The moral to the story is to trust God and take risks to advance his kingdom. Until I had worked with risk management and invested my own money, I never really understood this parable.

The whole bank risk project had two primary components, one headed by a colleague and the other which I headed, both of which supported Comptroller Eugene Ludwig's risk-based supervision initiative. My project focused on improving the bank failure model, which we developed in cooperation with the Federal Deposit Insurance Corporation (FDIC) and the Office of Management and Budget (OMB). This initial failure model yielded a probability of failure which tracked the historical performance of commercial bank failures well, but the FDIC customarily reported a higher number and rejected the model, which we wrote up and forgot about.

GFBA later focused on developing new models to support bank supervision and our deputy comptroller scheduled a week-long series of meetings to talk about it.

Why not program our existing bank failure model into a Windows program in a calculator format and simulate bank fail-

ure probabilities in real time? I thought as my mind wandered during these meetings.

I skipped out of the meeting on Monday, spent two and a half days programming, and returned on Wednesday to demonstrate my *"Bank Failure Calculator"* program.

The program generated instant buzz, although the group changed the name to *"Bank Calculator."* Over the next 7 years, I spent about half my time estimating new failure models.

The Tissue Box

When Christine entered third grade in 1998, Maryam and I wondered why she had not been placed in a new gifted and talented (GT) elementary school that opened in our area.

Few people who knew Christine doubted her exceptional abilities. At age three, she knew all her mathematics tables. At four, she memorized the Lord's Prayer on her own and recited it in Sunday school, unlike any other student. At five, she routinely memorized her piano music on first reading.

Christine's problem with piano proved unique because learning new music upset her and she cried her way through it. She cried so much that I kept a tissue box on top of the piano. Each time that I went over new music with her once, she cried and cried. After one hearing, she had memorized the music and could play it from memory. The crying arose because she never really learned to read music because her memory was so good.

In school, Christine's teachers typically used her as a teaching assistant because she learned so fast. She increasingly lost interest in classwork because she really needed to be in a more challenging program with other talented kids, as the GT program offered.

As we learned more about the GT program, we became aware that her teachers did not know that she was bilingual, speaking both English and Farsi. This oversight made a difference because bilingual students initially test out poorer than monolingual students in language skills, but catch up later and accelerate ahead of their peers. The program administrators accordingly score bilingual students differently than monolingual students in testing for the.GT program.

When Maryam and I met with her principal to point out that she was bilingual, the principal refused to acknowledge her error and accused us of disliking her new teacher, whom we hardly knew. We appealed Christine's case up to the county superintendent's office, but no one supported her appeal. The problem apparently was that bright students raised the average test scores for the schools that they attended and turf-conscious principals fought to keep them, rather than letting them go into the GT program, ignoring the best interest of the child.

After her principal retired, this problem went away and Christine entered the GT program in middle school. Being especially good in mathematics, Christine attended summer school to take the algebra class required to bring her into the highest track in mathematics and only offered only to students in the sixth grade at GT elementary schools.

Once in the GT program, Christine became a relentless student, studying all the time. She later competed successfully to attend Thomas Jefferson (TJ) High School that specializes in science, technology, engineering, and mathematics (STEM) studies and frequently ranks as the number one high school in the United States. After graduating from TJ, Christian went on to study mathematics and chemistry at Johns Hopkins University in Baltimore, Maryland, where she graduated in 2012.

Boundaries Revisited

*I*n the summer of 2002 at Centreville Presbyterian Church, Pastor Rob preached a sermon about personal boundaries that referred to a book, *Boundaries,* by Henry Cloud and John Townsend, who wrote:

> *Just as homeowners set out physical property lines around their land, we need to set mental, physical, emotional, and spiritual boundaries for our lives to help us distinguish what is our responsibility and what isn't. (25)*

Intrigued about the concept of boundaries, I bought and read the book.

Cloud and Townsend impressed me with two points.

The first point arose from Cloud and Townsend's reading of the story of the Good Samaritan (Luke 10:30–35) where they ask: why do we call the Samaritan good rather than great? The Samaritan saved the life of the man assaulted by robbers and cared for him (this made him *"good"*), but the Samaritan only took care of the man for a day before he delegated the man's care to an innkeeper and continued his trip. In other words, the Good Samaritan did what he could, but he balanced his care giving with other obligations.

This balancing of care giving and other obligations spoke

to my anxiety about being unable to solve the world food problem that left me feeling powerless to take steps of Christian charity within my reach. Recognizing my own limitations, I suddenly felt empowered to take the steps that I could. While I still lacked the power save the world, I could offer charity to the needy person standing in front of me. From that point forward, I began engaging street people outside my office in conversation. When panhandlers asked me for money, I routinely gave them twenty dollars, which invariably opened eyes, invited relationship, and led to conversation: why are you doing this? Even my colleagues noticed.

The second point arose from Cloud and Townsend's discussion of abuse, which they defined as disrespect for other people's boundaries. Our responsibility lies in communicating our boundaries; their responsibility lies in respecting those boundaries. Both parties share responsibility for healthy boundaries, which remains important in reducing the relational uncertainty that often causes pain, anxiety, and stress. Healing and joy spring from establishing healthy boundaries.

This definition of abuse countered my intuition. I remember working years earlier for a manager who threw a loud tantrum if you offended his sensibilities. After experiencing a couple of these tantrums, I went to a friend who knew him better to ask how she could work with him. She responded that she really enjoyed working with him because he was consistent. Once you recognized his hot buttons, relating to him posed no problem. In other words, my screaming manager had well-formed boundaries and, contrary to my initial impression, his staff did not perceive him as abusive.

This discussion of abuse alerted me to my own boundary-management problems at home and in the office.

At home, I volunteered to serve as an elder at church in the fall of 2002, which enhanced my sense of self-control over my time. During my three-year term as elder, our associate pastor resigned and Pastor Rob asked elders to offer personal testimonies on Sunday morning to give him some time off. While I found giving a testimonial uncomfortable, over the next year I began preaching quarterly.

In the office, I had a supervisor who routinely interrupted meetings to assert his business without regard for his staff. When I asked him to show common courtesy and not interrupt meetings, he took personal offense and placed me on a performance plan that took the form of a series of short-term research projects under tight supervision. Projects that others might complete over several months, I had to complete in about six weeks.

When an Indian colleague of mine faced the same dilemma, he filed a racial discrimination lawsuit. In my case, I focused on cranking out half a dozen studies for internal publication. But the plan was designed to encourage me to retire early. When I became eligible to retire in December 2003, I took the hint and applied for early retirement. Then, I retired from the Office of the Comptroller of the Currency (OCC) on a Friday in January 2004.

The following Monday I interviewed for a software consulting position. Over the next several months, I studied Koine Greek, which would permit me to read the New Testament in the original language, and interviewed for other consulting assignments. In June I found an assignment and applied for a full-time position as a financial engineer with the Office of Federal Housing Enterprise Oversight (OFHEO). When the OFHEO position came through in August, I negotiated a thirty-percent increase in salary over my OCC salary based on my pay rate as a consultant, an unexpected windfall.

Because of my windfall, the sequence of events—sermon heard, boundaries established, windfall received, preaching initiated—began to weigh on my mind. I also remembered my prayer in 1992 over my son's hospital bed: *"Lord, do not take him, take me."* I felt both God's provision and call.

Maryam viewed things differently. Responding to a call to ministry would involve setting aside a good-paying position to pay tuition and attend seminary. This appeared financially foolish and offered no guarantee of future employment. Lacking her support, I continued my work and put my kids through college.

PART 4: FULLY PRESENT

JOURNEY TO SEMINARY
Return to Leadership

*M*y term as ruling elder began in January 2003 when Centreville Presbyterian Church ordained me and I was elected as clerk of session. As clerk, I worked closely with the pastor to set agendas for the session and congregational meetings, and kept the official record of meetings.

Pastor Rob encouraged the elders to deepen their faith and to become more involved in the life of the church. At our monthly meetings, this encouragement took the form of dedicating the first half-hour to study and prayer. Oswald Sanders' book, *Spiritual Leadership*, which we studied together, made the point that elders needed to offer both spiritual and business leadership to the church.

Pastor Rob also encouraged us was to become more involved in the life of the church through preaching and teaching. That spring, our associate pastor resigned and Pastor Rob asked that elders offer personal testimonies on Sunday morning to give him some time off.

"I feel uncomfortable giving a personal testimonial, but if you want, I will preach for you. I am used to teaching college stu-

dents so it should be no problem to preach." I told him after initially avoiding the request.

"*Okay. Here's a book, Communicating for a Change, with me by Andy Stanley and Lane Jones that you might find helpful in getting started,*" *h*e told me.

Over the next year, I preached four times on the call to faith and ministry, the problem of pain, the Book of Esther, and the covenants of law and grace.

The following year, I taught my first adult Sunday school class, a video series crafted around R.C. Sproul's book: *Reason to Believe*. Because of the success of the class, in 2005 I was encouraged to teach Bible studies, starting with the Book of Romans. After that I taught Luke, Genesis, Hebrews, Philippians, and Matthew.

After a point in teaching, I got frustrated by the poor attendance on Sunday mornings.

Where are the elders? Where are the deacons? I thought.

Looking around the room, only one or two in a class of a dozen were even church members. Most were family members, colleagues from work, and active, non-members who wandered in. These were people who, like myself, struggled to understand and live out their faith during challenging times.

Mentor

*I*n the fall of 2003 my mentor at Michigan State University, Glenn L. Johnson, broke his hip removing a fallen tree from his back yard. Glenn knew me as well as anyone having served on my doctoral committee, attended the same church, and become a close friend during my student years. When I heard of his injury, he was in physical therapy and I called to check on him.

Among agricultural economists, Glenn was known for his work on the asset-fixity problem. This problem arises because, once investments in real capital are made, they cannot be reallocated without suffering a capital loss. Farmers continue producing at a loss, which, in the aggregate, leads to further price declines and worse losses. The asset-fixity problem provides a theoretical justification for farm policy intervention, which made Glenn's work famous.

Behind the asset-fixity problem is the stark reality of farm policy—modern agriculture produces too much food. The world food problem that motivated me to enter agricultural economics proved to be more about power politics than about food production constraints. When farmers in the developed countries produce too much food due to subsidies, low food prices force farmers in developing countries into poverty. When I realized that the world food problem was a modern myth, I also knew that agricultural economics could not be my ultimate call as a Christian.

Professionals face the same asset-fixity problem when they invest years of work in a particular field, only to find their work ignored and their career stalled. For both the farmer and the professional, the problem of getting stuck is best solved by investing in new skills and activities during slow periods. As the saying goes, you have to know when to cut bait and when to go fishing.

During my conversation with Glenn, we talked about my work at OCC on agricultural banking, but I also regaled him with details of a sermon that I spent weeks preparing. On and on I went about this sermon, getting more excited by the minute.

"Stephen, you really seem to enjoy preaching, why don't you go to seminary?" Glenn blurted out after listening patiently for several minutes.

Stunned. I thanked him and excused myself.

After several months passed, I heard through the grapevine that Glenn passed away the week after I spoke with him.

Stephen...why don't you go to seminary? Stephen...why don't you go to seminary? Glenn's words kept going through my head like Jesus' last words to Peter: *"Feed my sheep . . . feed my sheep"* (John 21:15).

Visit to Princeton

*A*fter retiring from the Office of the Comptroller of the Currency in January 2004, I attended an inquirer's weekend held at Princeton Theological Seminary (PTS) in Princeton, New Jersey for those *"inquiring"* into a career in ministry. PTS put me up in their guest house and the program included faculty talks, meetings with admissions counselors, and visits to classes, including a preaching class. Before the weekend was over, my hair was on fire for the Lord and I fell in love with PTS oblivious to challenges that I encountered during the visit.

One challenge occurred during lunch on Friday in the cafeteria when I overlooked the discomfort that some of the twenty-something year old students had eating with someone twice their age. Out of an inquiry group of sixty, I was older than both visitors and faculty, who seemed unprepared for my questions.

"Why does the Bible refer to Jesus rather than his given name, Jeshua?" I asked having wondered about it for years.

Later in seminary I learned that Greek has no *"shu"* sound like in Hebrew.

Another challenge arose in Friday chapel when a senior preached about an evangelism experience that consisted of boldly wearing a PTS t-shirt on the New York subway. He then proceeded to ridicule apologetics, the primary interest I expressed on my PTS application.

I later learned that PTS offered no classes in apologetics and that their commitment to theological diversity consisted primarily of hiring faculty who self-identified as liberal or evangelical in their research interests. Practical experience in missions or evangelism was not required.

Still another challenge arose when PTS offered a dinner Friday evening in which the dean invited each inquirer to introduce themselves and talk about their call to ministry. One person after another described a meaningful high school young group experience that led them to consider pastoring a church. When my turn came, I described tension between a call to ministry and the financial need to support a reluctant family.

Probably the biggest challenge arose on Friday evening after dinner, when inquirers were given a choice between attending a play called the *Vagina Monologues* and a film, *The Passion of the Christ*. The *Vagina Monologues* focused on:

> *consensual and nonconsensual sexual experiences, body image, genital mutilation, direct and indirect encounters with reproduction, sex work, and several other topics through the eyes of women with various ages, races, sexualities, and other differences.*

The Passion of the Christ focused on the suffering of Christ during his trial and execution on the cross. Two out of sixty of us chose the film. Discussions with students assigned to attend the film with us highlighted the theological divide between those in the church focused on gender politics and those focused on the Gospel, but it took lengthy reflection on this divide to understand its significance for my own ministry.

On returning home, I completed my PTS application, but I withdrew it later in the summer after being offered a position as a financial engineer at Office of Federal Housing Enterprise Oversight (OFHEO). Because PTS lacked a part-time study program, I could not both work and attend seminary.

While I had worked for about a decade to prepare for and apply for a position at OFHEO, taking the position caused me great anxiety. I had dreamed of being a full-time financial engineer since my days in Farm Credit Administration, yet I felt that I had betrayed my call to ministry in accepting this position. Over the next several years, I despaired over my inability to attend seminary full-time and began visiting other seminaries. I also began studying Greek and Hebrew, and continued to teach adult Bible studies at Centreville Presbyterian Church.

Diane's Passing

*I*n 2006, my sister, Diane, developed a second round of breast cancer. She started chemo-therapy unsuccessfully in the fall and planned a new round of chemo in the New Year. After Christmas I drove to Philadelphia to visit her and offer encouragement.

When I arrived, we walked around the house inspecting the renovations that she had completed. She was especially proud of her new kitchen that included a system of warm water circulation in the floor tiling.

I bought her a DVD film starring Queen Latifah, *Last Holiday*, which we watched together. The film is the story of a woman, Georgia, who was diagnosed with a fatal neurological disorder and decides to blow her life savings on visiting a celebrity chef working in a large, luxury hotel, called the Grand Hotel Pupp in the Czech Republic. During her visit, Georgia discovers hidden talents, finds love, and, in the end, learns that she had been misdiagnosed. I expected the film would offer Diane hope and the strength to persevere in her new chemo treatments.

On Monday, February 12, 2007, my mother called me at six-thirty in the morning, as I commuted to work in Washington

D.C. with a colleague.

"Diane is asking for her brothers," my mother told me.

"How is she?" I asked.

"Diane had a stroke and a heart attack last night."

What had begun days earlier as an adverse reaction to chemo, had by Sunday night left Diane unconscious.

I returned to Centreville, dropped off my colleague, and picked up John. Together, we then traveled to Springfield, Pennsylvania, where Diane lay in the intensive care unit of a local hospital. Our parents, who had traveled earlier in the week to visit Diane, were waiting for us.

When John and I arrived at the hospital mid-morning, Diane lay unresponsive on life-support and no longer looked like the person that I remembered. The doctors said that nothing further could be done. I consoled my brother-in-law, Hugo, while we waited for their pastor to arrive. Then, we read Psalm 23 and prayed. After our brief service together, we instructed the doctor to remove Diane from life support and sat with her as she took her last breaths.

Hugo and my father worked to schedule funeral services for Thursday at Diane's home church, First Presbyterian Church, in Springfield, Pennsylvania and for Saturday at Lewinsville Presbyterian Church (LPC) in McLean, Virginia, where Diane would also be interned in the family burial plot. I thought to attend just the LPC service, but my father insisted that I eulogize Diane at both services.

As I prepared my eulogy, I realized that Diane and our cousin, Carol Snook, the two, closest friends of my youth, had preceded me in death even though I had preceded them in life. Carol died years earlier at the age of 31 of an undiagnosed heart condition leaving behind John and Jackie, ages three and four; Diane left behind a teen-aged son, William, who grieved fiercely. My own grief ran silent and deep. The passing of Diane and Carol brought my mortality more clearly into view, sharpening my sense of urgency in attending to life's work.

At the Springfield service the church was packed with roughly 350 people attending, but the only people that I knew were family members and my friend, Jon, from high school, who pastors a Lutheran church in Pennsylvania. As I grieved Diane, I was surprised to draw comfort from the fellowship of the strangers present that night. At the McLean service, as I looked out from the pulpit, I could see the entire Hiemstra family, many friends in Christ, and about a dozen friends from my office.

The LPC service was the first time many friends and colleagues had seen me take the pulpit and it served as a *"Wedding at Cana"* moment in my ministry. Just as Jesus' mother, Mary, drafted her reluctant son into solving the wine problem at Cana, my father had pushed me to eulogize Diane both in Springfield and McLean.

After the McLean service, I noticed that the colleagues who saw me in the pulpit and heard my eulogy stopped using profanity in my presence. I was sensitive to this change, because I struggled to clean up my own language.

Over the following year, I also changed my attitude about part-time seminary studies and in March of 2008 I drove to Charlotte, North Carolina with a friend to attend an open house at Gordon-Conwell Theological Seminary (GCTS). Walking through the door, GCTS students greeted us and we felt truly welcomed seeing many second career students and learning that the entire curriculum could be taken during long weekend visits. Unlike other seminaries, at GCTS we could work and study, which was critical for both of us.

Also unlike other seminaries that I visited, African Americans made up about a third of the GCTS students, while seminarians of color were largely absent on other campuses. Having worked in Washington D.C. for twenty-seven years, I had many

African American colleagues and respected their deep spirituality. Seeing the African American students at GCTS gave me comfort that I had finally found the right seminary home.

When I returned to my home in Centreville, I applied to GCTS, was accepted and began classes the following August. I never experienced such joy as I felt on entering seminary.

Changes in Routine

Between February 1984 and May 2007, I journaled episodically recording major life events. On October 4, 2000, for example, I recorded the death of my grandfather, Frank Hiemstra and the next event, May 13, 2003, I recorded that my son, Stephen Reza, had given his life to Christ. This pattern of journaling persisted for many years.

In 2006, Pastor Neil Craigan at Centreville Presbyterian Church experimented with holding a Saturday evening service, Soul Café focused on church workers, who seldom got a moment's peace on Sunday mornings. Soul Café began around 5:30 p.m. when coffee was served, he pulled up a stool, and began talking. The Hiemstra family attended this service weekly, but it never caught on with the rest of the congregation and eventually it was dropped.

My morning routine began to evolve in 2007 after I read a book—Eugene Peterson's *Eat This Book*—that Pastor Neil Craigan had thrown to me during one of these Saturday services the previous fall.

The book was an eye-opener. Among other things, it outlined the spiritual practice of *"Lectio Divina"* and the connection of the title to Revelation 10:9:

> *So I went to the angel and told him to give me*
>
> *the little scroll. And he said to me,*
>
> *Take and eat it; it will make your stomach bitter,*
>
> *but in your mouth it will be sweet as honey.*

Studying this book, I became convinced of the need to add a series of spiritual practices, including journaling, Bible study, and daily examinen, to my daily prayer.

On May 4th, 2007, my journaling pattern changed as I noted in my journal:

> *In the New Year, I began Hebrew class as the Jewish Community Center. The class ran ten weeks. My goal was to learn to read the Hebrew alphabet so that I could study further on my own [as I had for Greek since 2004]. In mid-March, I then began reading Genesis [in Hebrew]. While Hebrew is entirely new to me, for a long while I had a strange sense of deja vue about the language.*

At first, I journaled more frequently but by July 15th I was making daily entries. I started getting up a half hour earlier before work at 4 a.m. to make this new routine possible. This routine quickly morphed into praying continuously throughout the day.

Looking the Part

Seminary students must grow academically and relationally which requires changes in both the student and the community. Pastors both work for their congregations and lead them in a covenant relationship, where one cares for the other. This relationship can, however, get complicated.

When I entered seminary and became an inquirer with National Capital Presbytery, I served as a ruling elder at Centreville Presbyterian (CPC) on session, the ruling board for the church. Each elder had an assignment and my assignment involved serving as clerk of session, which meant that I worked closely with the pastor to plan session agendas, keep session records, and keep track of official correspondence. Because both the pastor and session serve as mentors to inquirers and candidates of ministry, my roles conflicted—it is hard to mentor oneself. This conflict proved stressful and within a few months I resigned from the clerk's role and from session.

The role conflict between clerk of session and pastor in training symbolized a larger identity transition that I was going through in seminary. As elder and clerk, my leadership role focused on technical competence in managing the business affairs of the church, as exemplified by my work as an economist. As pastor in training, my leadership role focused on developing my relational competence. While inwardly I felt this transition proceeding daily through my seminary studies and pastoral work, externally these changes appeared less obvious to people who have known me for decades but did not work with me day to day. The question arose: how do I get people to reboot their image of me, from economist to pastor?

In the summer of 2009, CPC invited five former members who had been called into ordained pastoral ministry back to the church to preach a sermon series on God's call; as a seminary student, the pastor also invited me to preach on August 23. In view of my struggle with pastoral identity, I enlisted the assistance of a couple of friends to introduce the sermon with a little skit designed to kill off the *"Dr. Hiemstra"* persona at CPC:

"Is this going to be one of those boring sermons that you just read?" Heckler said from the back of the room.

"This?" I held up the script.

"Put it right in here," heckler holds up a trash can.

I ripped up the script and deposited it in the can.

Heckler walked off a few steps . . .

I smiled and pulled out a backup script.

"Oh no you don't," heckler returned with the trash can.

I ripped up the second script. Then, stood holding my jacket lapels and smiling . . .

"Do you think you can be a pastor by dressing the part?" Asked the second heckler.

I pointed to myself.

"You don't need a suit coat to be a pastor—what you need is a call from God," heckler said and paused. *"Here take this,"* heckler tossed me a CPC t-shirt.

I took off my jacket and put on the t-shirt.

"Someone warned me that ministry is a team sport at CPC!" I concluded.

After a prayer, I preached on the story of Stephen, the first Christian martyr, in Acts chapter seven, which was my first sermon preached without notes.

After the sermon, my mother asked for my new CPC t-shirt and I gave it to her. The sermon itself softened my pastoral image and eight years later friends and family still remind me of it.

TRAVELING PARTNERS

My Diet

*A*s a junior at Westfield High School in the fall of 2008, my son, Stephen Reza, started to think about graduation and college. Christine had graduated the previous June from Thomas Jefferson High School and had just started college at Johns Hopkins University; Narsis would be graduating the following June. As he contemplated college, he introduced himself more and more as just Reza.

Reza was a disciplined kid. He enjoyed piano and never needed to be reminded to practice or to study. He also ate like his mother, never eating an extra bite and always keeping himself fit. Reza looked and dressed like a model for *Gentlemen's Quarterly*. This discipline served him well over the years because having only a single, partially-functioning kidney meant that he followed doctor's orders, took his pills on time, and successfully delayed dialysis until high school.

Peritoneal dialysis is a pain. Reza had surgery to insert a tube into his peritoneal, the lining around the vital organs, and that tube had to remain absolutely sterile or a life-threatening infection could spring up in a matter of hours. Twice that winter we had emergency visits to Fairfax Hospital where we would be admitted and, then, have to wait in the emergency department until the department contacted on-call nephrologist for advice— normal nurses and doctors are unfamiliar with the drill for dialysis emergencies. Day-to-day peritoneal dialysis requires a strict bed-time schedule and Reza had to remain in bed all night attached to a machine the size of a laptop computer that pumped fluid in and out of his peritoneal while he slept. Our closets were full of bags of this fluid, which was delivered monthly.

"Dad. I am tired of dialysis. How come I can't just get a kidney transplant? Is it just a money thing?"

"Rez. You know the story. You can only stay on our medical plan until age twenty-three and you won't even be out of college. After that, medicare pays for dialysis, but will only pay for the transplant and three years of anti-rejection medication. It is better to wait until you are twenty-three to start that clock."

"I just want to enjoy college without worrying about dialysis and having a tube sticking out of my gut."

Up until that winter, Reza trusted my judgment. When his trust started to wane, I decided to proceed with transplantation, without knowing whether a kidney could be found for him or how to pay for his medications. I put myself on a strict diet with the intention of donating one of my own kidneys and lost over twenty pounds over the coming months.

We went to visit the transplant specialist associated with Inova Fairfax Hospital.

"What took you so long?" The doctor asked me.

"Huh? What do you mean?" I responded.

"What took you so long to request a transplant? Most patients come to me the moment that they go on dialysis. You waited two years."

"Dialysis was working for us, but Reza wanted to have transplant in time for college."

As we soon learned, pediatric dialysis patients are at high risk of suicide, something we were never told. Reza's ability to tolerate dialysis put him *"off the Richter scale"* as a disciplined young man. Most young people who come to dialysis are born without a kidney problem, but develop a problem, like diabetes, that leaves them without proper kidney function; therefore, dialysis comes an alienating addition to an already stressful life and it freaks them out. For Reza, chronic kidney issues were always a fact of life.

When it came time for me to donate my kidney in June, I was given a sonogram. I learned that I had two healthy kidneys, but I was ineligible to donate because my kidneys had two blood vessels feeding them, not one. This condition, known as a polar kidney, makes transplantation difficult because one vessel is too small to reconnect, which results in a loss of kidney tissue. The news devastated us, because it left Reza with no obvious transplant partner—Maryam had just recovered from breast cancer and was also ineligible to transplant.

Monday, July 14th, while working at home, I received a call from the transplant center. A young Hispanic man had died the night before in a car accident and was a match for Reza. I picked up Reza from school and drove to Inova Fairfax Hospital where we checked in together. Late that night, Reza had surgery. We spent two nights in the pediatric intensive care unit before being transported in the middle of the night to a private room, where we spent the remainder of the week.

When it was over, Reza was able to start his senior year fully recovered and able to focus on his studies. Ever-disciplined, he takes his pills like clockwork.

In March 2010, The Affordable Care Act was signed into law and the financial dilemma that we had faced in seeking transplantation was eliminated by allowing kids to remain on their parent's medical plans until age 26.

A Difficult Trip

I came to love the monthly drive west of Centreville out interstate 66 to interstate 81 south which connects to interstate 77 and travels all the way to Charlotte, NC, where I attended seminary. Interstate 81 passed close by Radford University and Virginia Tech where Narsis and Reza attended college. During seminary, I stopped by Radford for lunch with Narsis on Fridays and stopped by Blacksburg for dinner with Reza on Saturday evenings. All through their college years I got to see my kids more often than others in the family. Although Reza was the youngest, *Nars* was the sensitive child and daddy's little girl.

Driving down interstate 81, I ruminated on how each of the three children played piano from the age of five. By high school, each of the kids had performed in music festivals for six and seven years with distinction, but Nars out-shined her brother and sister at the keyboard. Like my mother, Nars had a heart for music and taught herself to play guitar with minimal encouragement.

In spite of her obvious musical talent, in high school Narsis lost all interest in music and her studies, and started misbehaving. By her senior year of high school, Narsis was unsure that she wanted to attend college, but fell in love with Radford University when we visited campus together.

Several weeks before traveling to Radford, I dreamed that I walked down a road and came across a mudslide, as in California foothills after a heavy rain. Curious, I walked up the hill overlooking the mudslide and, looked down. There I saw a man in the debris preoccupied with a large, flat stone—a headstone, which he kept turning over. As he turned this headstone over, he sank deeper and deeper into the debris.

"Forget the stone; get out of there!" I screamed.

He ignored me and continued turning the stone over until he disappeared into the mud. As he sank out of sight, three spotlessly, white figures arose out of the mudslide.

"A man sunk down into the mud there; get him out!" I called out to them, pointing to where the man had been.

They rescued the man and I woke up.

The trip from Centreville to Radford, Virginia takes about four-hours, but I hardly noticed as my mind wandered to the events leading up to this mid-semester trip in March 2010. After arriving in Radford, I loaded Nars' things into our blue Sienna minivan while she cleaned the room.

When we finished, I asked her to pray with me, something I had not done before. I praised God for my daughter; I asked God's forgiveness for my shortcomings as a parent; I thanked God for her life; and, at the end of it, I asked God for her deliverance. For twenty minutes, I poured myself out in tearful prayer and, when I finished, I had no energy left. I asked Nars to drive and fell asleep as we set off north on Interstate 81.

About twenty minutes later, I heard a crash and woke to see a passing eighteen-wheeler clip a car in front of us. The car deflected into the right guard rail; exploded into pieces; and went into a spin into left lane straight at us. Traveling at sixty-five miles per hour, Nars swerved the van onto the left shoulder, throwing up gravel as we went. Looking out the front window, three terrified passengers in the car spun, passing within inches of my minivan door. Their car came to a stop behind us in the left lane again facing north again with the traffic. Shaken; we pulled over about a hundred yards further up the highway. Nars and I exchanged silent glances for a second. Gathering my senses, I jumped out and sprinted back to the car where the three occupants sat stunned, but miraculously unhurt.

"Are you okay?" I asked.

"Yes," they whispered, nodding.

As an ambulance pulled up to offer assistance, I turned and walked back to the car. Nars' eyes met me with a shaken look.

"Everyone is okay." I reported.

"Good."

Slowly, She started the van and began to concentrate on driving again. She pulled back onto the highway and headed north towards Roanoke. For the remainder of the trip, conversation seemed pointless.

The Goads

*F*riends in Christ who know Maryam understand why I fell in love with her.

"You won the lottery when you married me," Maryam frequently reminds me in a very Iranian turn of phrase.

Still, many ask how my marriage to a Muslim has informed my faith and call to ministry, a question required greater self-knowledge and theological depth than I could muster for many years.

When Maryam and I became engaged in 1984, I asked her to attend church, which she did faithfully until our kids grew up and attended college. I was confident that in attending church the Holy Spirit would work in Maryam's life to bring her to faith in Jesus Christ. As time passed, however, I became increasingly convicted of my negligence as a witness and began to explore my own faith more deeply, hoping to become a better witness.

Our kids always attended church and Sunday school growing up. Evenings at home, I held family Bible studies and I took the kids to piano lessons and youth group programs. As I witnessed to them, my faith blossomed, even as Maryam remained a Muslim.

Stubborn as I was, I failed to recognize God's call on my life; God used my wife to goad me out of an idolatrous relationship with my work and to bring me closer to him. The Bible illustrates a similar process at work in the story of the Prophet Hosea, who also married an improbable wife, Gomer, whose sin God used to highlight the idolatry of the Nation of Israel (Hos 1:2–3).

Idolatry also figured prominently in the call of the Apostle Paul, whom the risen Christ accused of kicking against the goads, as cited above. Paul describes himself before he came to faith in Christ as:

> *If anyone else thinks he has reason for confidence in the flesh, I have more: circumcised on the eighth day, of the people of Israel, of the tribe of Benjamin, a Hebrew of Hebrews; as to the law, a Pharisee; as to zeal, a persecutor of the church; as to righteousness under the law, blameless.* (Phil 3:4–6)

Paul's idolatry took the form of being zealous for the law and the trappings of religion, but being tone-deaf to the voice of the Holy Spirit.

When we zealously prosecute the law—beit Mosaic, Islamic, secular, or physical law—rather than worship almighty God who created the law, we commit idolatry. Or when we work zealously and worship God sparingly, as I did, we commit idolatry and come under judgment, as we know from the first commandment: *"You shall have no other gods before me."* (Exod 20:3) Even if we ignore of the problem of idolatry and suffer blindly in our ignorance, God sees our shortcomings.

In the context of a highly secularized society and syncretistic church, anyone who takes God seriously today has to be considered a brother or sister in the faith—Islam is not a threat to our faith. Rather, Islam reminds us of God's transcendence while many Christians obsess about Christ's immanence and neglect his divinity. The threat to the church is that we have forgotten who we are and whose we are, and treat our faith as one of a host of priorities, as evidenced from my own history.

For many years, I believed that I attended seminary in spite of my wife, but I came to understand that I attended seminary because of my wife. I now know that God placed Maryam in my life to goad me into a a healthier marriage, a deeper faith, and a call to ministry.

EARLY MINISTRY

Oaks of Righteousness

*I*n 2010 my ordination committee requested that I volunteer as a pastoral intern outside of my home church. Having never interned, I emailed the General Presbyter to request placement in an urban congregation and he emailed my request to half a dozen pastors. Among these pastors, only Pastor Chris responded and he quickly arranged for me to visit First Presbyterian Church of Annandale (FPCA).

Before my visit, I thought that I knew Annandale. In the late 1970s, when my sister, Diane, and her husband, Hugo, purchased a garden condominium on Americana Drive in Annandale could be described as an affordable, up-and-coming, suburban town with good schools inside the Washington D.C. Beltway. Later in the early 1980s, when my other sister, Karen, and her husband, Doug, joined them, the picture remained much the same.

But, when I visited Annandale in May of 2010, my memories of the area had grown stale and I had trouble finding Americana Drive. The bushes and bedding plants around the houses appeared untended and overgrown. Even the pavement on the main thoroughfare, Little River Turnpike, looked as worn out as the people who lived there. In place of crew-cut veterans, on the streets walked white-haired and balding seniors; in place of teenagers hanging out in front of the McDonalds stood Hispanic day-workers. The up and coming suburb that I remembered had aged and suffered urban blight.

Driving up Newcastle Drive, the grounds of the brick church greeted me with enormous oaks, marked out and steady. Unsteady trees, like white pine or popular, can grow thirty to forty feet in a few years, but steadiness requires the patience of an oak. Formative white oak—faithfully rooted, humbly set— guarded the FPCA spire, as I parked my car behind the church.

At the end of the long, winding driveway, FPCA offered many doors to enter the building and, for those in need, the shelter of a roof on rainy days. Sunshine, not rain, greeted me during my first visit and I instinctively ducked under the roof to enter the door that leads to the sanctuary.

In the sanctuary, a large white Celtic cross on fire with an avian image of the Holy Spirit hung behind a wooden pulpit. To the left of the cross, red and yellow stained glass windows radiated light but to the right of the cross, a wooden pipe organ captured my attention. Baptized in the shadow of an organ, confirmed by a Handel chorus, and served communion by piped melodies while my mother still cradled me in her arms, memories of organ music overpowered me. Before speaking a word, I felt at home in FPCA.

Before I found him, Pastor Chris found me. We toured the many classrooms, the day-care center, the kitchen, the library, and the staff offices. With the facility came a church's proud history—the building was dedicated in 1960 and expanded in 1963; by 1970, the church had 575 children in Sunday school; two years later membership peaked at 883 active members; and in 1974 the organ was added. More recent history, however, piqued my interest. The church had evolved partnerships with First Korean Presbyterian Church of Virginia (since 1965) and a Pakistani mission congregation, like few other congregations. And each congregation partnered together with the others in worship, programming, and budget.

Hooked. I joined the staff and interned at FPCA over the next year.

Pastoral Intern

During the fall of 2010, I interned with the First Presbyterian Church of Annandale (FPCA) where I was given an office and a mailbox, and attended staff meetings on Mondays, my flex day.

FPCA reminded me of Riverdale Presbyterian Church, the church that I grew up in. Both congregation loved choral and pipe organ music and both shared educational buildings with the same painted cinder-block construction. Each Sunday Pastor Chris preached the lectionary in his doctoral robe to a congregation of about eighty, mostly retired civil servants.

As the weeks passed, I discovered that I loved working with the older people. I taught an adult Sunday school class in the fall and preached about once a month. At FPCA I distinguished myself as the first pastor to the leave the pulpit, walk down the aisle, and preach without notes in a clerical collar.

Maryam occasionally attended FPCA with the kids and especially enjoyed the Christmas Eve service when we held a joint service with three international churches: the Koreans, the Pakistanis, and the Indonesians. Parts of the service were in four languages. More generally, Maryam preferred the praise music over the choral and organ music and a younger congregation, like our home church in Centreville.

At the end of October, FPCA's partner church, the First Korean Church of Virginia Presbyterian Church, hosted a Halloween celebration for children in the neighborhood. They rented a moon-bounce, provided goodies, led games, and introduced kids to the Gospel. The response was encouraging, but about forty Hispanic kids showed up who spoke mostly Spanish and none of the adults present spoke Spanish.

Over the next few weeks, there was much hand-wringing over this lost ministry opportunity. As the only member of the staff who spoke even a little Spanish, I was embarrassed to learn about this event second-hand. I was also embarrassed to have to explain the limitations on my fluency. My Spanish vocabulary focused on words interesting to an agricultural economist, not a pastor addressing issues of faith, because I had not attended church often when I lived in Puerto Rico. An important opportunity to connect with the community withered for lack of ministry capability.

Providence Hospital

*I*n 2010 when I began interning with First Presbyterian Church of Annandale (FPCA), I worked full-time as a financial engineer at the Federal Housing Enterprise Agency (FHFA) and traveled for classes once a month to Gordon-Conwell Theological Seminary (GCTS) in Charlotte, NC. The excitement that year energized me, but the frantic pace also proved unsustainable.

In FHFA, I worked to model the capital adequacy of Freddie Mac and Fannie Mae (The Enterprises) through the use of a large income and balance sheet model, known as the Risk Based Capital model (RBC). In the second half of 2010, I developed a guarantee fee model for the enterprises, the first of its kind in the public sector, and an important first step in developing an alternative to the RBC, which was stripped out of regulatory use with legislation passed in 2008.

By the fall, I found myself needing to take annual leave to finish papers and attend class. I requested permission to work a four-ten-hour day schedule to make better use of my commuting time and allow time to study, but my request was repeatedly denied. I continued to push myself too hard and began to have anxiety issues, until on December 4, 2010, I filed the paperwork to retire from FHFA at year's end. The following week, FHFA announced that my office would be eliminated on the same day!

I began 2011 as a full-time seminary student. To honor my ordination committee's request that I take clinical pastoral education (CPE), I signed up to join a CPE group at Providence Hospital in Northeast Washington D.C., which serves primarily Medicare patients in Washington's African American community. I requested assignment to Seton House, the hospital's psychiatric ward, to perform my duties as a chaplain intern. My request was granted, but my time would be divided between Seton House and the emergency department, as was customary for interns.

CPE instructs pastors in pastoral care through self-knowledge, instruction, group therapy, and the case study method. In the first unit, students do such things as write a personal history, learn about emotional intelligence and active listening, and visit with patients. Students are encouraged to write case studies of problematic visits to solicit feedback in group from other students and the instructor.

One goal of CPE instruction is to learn to be fully present in conversations with patients and other people. Fully present means attentively listening when patient's talk to identify their deep concerns and focus on them. People instinctively tell their stories, but the emotional content is often hidden in conversation. By learning the basic story types, pastors can quickly identify the stories being told and focus on them.

A common story type is a transition, which has three parts—a beginning, middle, and end. The basic hospital visit is a transition.

What brings you to the hospital today? Or, how is your hospital stay going? Or, what happens when you leave the hospital? I might ask.

Each question focuses on a different part of the transition and provides insight into how the patient is coping.

Self-knowledge is surprisingly important in pastoral visits. If you have an unresolved, painful experience in your past, a patient visit could bring it up again and trigger an emotional reaction that distracts from the visit, something known as an emotional hijacking.

One morning in the emergency department, the charge nurse sent me to visit with a young woman who had just spontaneously aborted her pregnancy. She was still in pain and sat in a private room with her mother. I ministered to her successfully for about fifteen minutes before it was obvious that we had reversed roles—she was ministering to me, not me to her.

As we talked about her pregnancy, I remembered how Maryam and I had lost our first pregnancy, which I never grieved properly. My visit with the young woman led me to feel my loss deeply—I experienced an emotional hijacking—and I had to break off my visit in the emergency room after twenty minutes. I left and went to the chapel to cry for half an hour, something out of character for me.

Before my time in CPE, I had been afraid to pray with strangers, but it proved easier than I had imagined. During my visits in the emergency department, I also learned that I have a high tolerance for chaos, which distinguished me from most other students. I also learned that I really enjoyed working with African Americans, who accepted me graciously.

My visits in Seton House could be drawn out over several days and often had more depth than visits in the emergency department. While patients stayed in the emergency department for a few hours and a few were placed in hospital rooms for a day or two, Seton patients normally stayed between three and fourteen days. I accordingly learned to pace my visits with Seton residents and might even devote study time to learning about particular afflictions before talking with the patient.

Each day in Seton House, I would ask to be briefed by

the charge nurse on new patients. Then, I reviewed the census, which listed patient name, age, diagnosis, and a few other details. After catching up, I sought to observe new patients in one of the groups that they participated in. The ward had, for example, groups to talk about how you are doing, art groups, news groups, and groups with particular staff members. Observing the groups, I would learn about patient demeanor, patterns of interaction with other patients, and, perhaps, what set them off.

One elderly patient, for example, often bragged about spending seven years in prison for murder, but would become combative if a staff member served him rice. Another patient from Eastern Europe drew detailed pictures of Nazi soldiers smoking cigarettes with burning villages in the background, but he never wanted to talk about what he had drawn.

One morning as an art group assembled to begin their work, attendance was especially heavy and I offered my chair to a latecomer who took offense and began escalating. As the staff gathered putting on their blue latex gloves to intervene, the other patients came to my defense saying—*"leave the pastor alone"*— and threatened the patient who was now shouting at full throttle. I was stunned for having been called out by the patient, but I was truly humbled by support given me by the other patients, something that I will never forget.

Hispanic Ministry

*I*n January 2011, when I interviewed with the director of pastoral care at Providence Hospital, the issue of Spanish fluency came up again.

"Steve, how would you feel about working in our maternity ward? I see from your resume that you lived in Puerto Rico and speak Spanish. About two-thirds of the women in the ward are Hispanic and we do not have anyone else in pastoral care who speaks Spanish," he asked me.

"I would be happy to work in the maternity ward, but you need to know that my Spanish is limited to basic conversation and the vocabulary used by economists, not pastors."

Thinking about the problem of a fifty-something-year-old man ministering in a maternity ward full of young women, I immediately ordered several clerical shirts and collars to preclude any ambiguity about my role in this setting. While the director graciously assigned me elsewhere, I quickly discovered that Hispanic ministry was unavoidable elsewhere in the hospital.

In the emergency department, I frequently found myself the only staff member talking to Hispanic men brought in by the emergency medical technicians (EMTs). Because the men often drank cheap liquor on Friday evenings and passed out in the street, the EMTs often knew these men and brought them in on Saturdays, knowing that they would end up dead if they persisted in this behavior. The hospital staff admitted them passed out or screaming and strapped them in a gurney until they sobered up. I was drawn to this patients because they disrupted other patients with their screaming and I had become the go-to guy for managing disruptive patients, because of my age and calm demeanor.

One Saturday afternoon as I made my rounds in the emergency department, I checked on a young woman who had been there most of the day.

"How is it going?" I asked.

"I have been trying to sleep while I wait to be seen, but this guy down the hall keeps waking me up with his screaming."

"Let me see what I can do."

The room had a hundred patients or more that afternoon so noise was unavoidable, but this man stood out. He lay on a gurney in the middle of the room. As I approached him, a nurse requested a urine sample from him so he stood up, unzipped his trousers, and filled up the beaker in front of everyone. He then laid back down on the gurney and started crying loudly. The man appeared about six feet tall; he was lean and muscular with a dark complexion, a hint of a mustache, and the careless attitude of a drunk.

"Hi. My name is Steve and I am with pastoral care. What seems to be the problem?"

"My brother died," he responded with a slight Spanish accent.

"Oh. When did he die?"

"He died five years ago when he was forty of alcohol abuse, just like my father."

Looking at him, the man appeared to be about forty.

"So your brother died at the age of forty and now you are forty and you think that you are now going to die?"

"Yes. Today is my birthday."

We hugged. Then, we began a serious discussion about how to get help for alcohol abuse. The key to having that discussion rested on understanding that he was experiencing an *"anniversary"* (an important story type) and being comfortable in talking with him in spite of his imposing stature and volatile emotional state.

Experiences like these led me to hear God calling me to

improve my Spanish.

When my year at First Presbyterian Church of Annandale (FPCA) was over and I graduated from my CPE class at Providence Hospital, I was exhausted. Working in the psychiatric ward, I learned to recognize the signs of addiction and realized that I was more than exhausted, I was stress addicted. One can be addicted to anything and the clearest sign of addiction is that you experience withdrawal symptoms when you give it up—I got anxious and upset when I I took off time and tried to relax. In response to this intuition, I said goodbye to FPCA in June 2011 and began practicing Sabbath rest.

In September 2011, I decided to attend Riverside Presbyterian Church (RPC) in Sterling, Virginia, which had an Hispanic congregation integrated with its English congregation. I planned to slip into the back row and worship with them quietly in Spanish, but this church had no back row! They embraced me wholeheartedly and, when they heard that I was a seminary student, they encouraged me to get involved in their ministry.

Later in the fall of 2011 as I drifted off in church listening to a sermon in Spanish, again I wondered whether I had made a mistake in choosing to get involved in Hispanic ministry.

"Lord, why have you brought me to this time and this

place." I prayed.

God answered my prayer reminding me how I had come to Christ through the testimony of a young New York gang member—Nicky Cruz—during a movie, *The Cross and the Switchblade.* I thought: Cruz, Cruz—that sounds Puerto Rican, which turned out to be correct. God led me to faith at age thirteen through the testimony of a young Puerto Rican, led me back to Puerto Rico in 1977, and led me to take up Hispanic ministry in 2011, all quite ignorant of his plan.

At the encouragement of my ordination committee, I later became a pastoral intern at RPC and began preaching and teaching in Spanish. Pastor Edwin Andrade, who grew up in Guatemala, encouraged me to write up my Sunday school lessons and distribute them to the congregation through email. Although I had written a newsletter at school and had written for the presbytery newsletter for five years, composing these Sunday school lessons in English and Spanish expanded both the content and frequency of my writing. It was a small step two years later to write my first book and, then, to translate it into Spanish.

EPILOGUE

344   *Called Along the Way*

*D*uring the Last Supper, Jesus explained to the disciples what would happen to him.

"Lord, we do not know where you are going. How can we know the way?" Thomas, the skeptic and standing for modern thinkers, asked him.

"I am the way, and the truth, and the life. No one comes to the Father except through me." (John 14:5–6) Jesus told him.

We often repeat this story at funerals because it is an interpretive key. When life is confusing, Jesus' words help us share our feelings and they guide our actions.

I often find that life appears most confusing when I fixate too much on the present, forget my own history, and lose sight of the future. As Christians, we know that our future is in Christ and because we know the end of the story, we also know that present afflictions are temporary, not the end of the story. The past reminds us of the many afflictions that we have already overcome, God's gracious work in our lives, and the many blessings that God has given us.

For me, this memoir has given life to these memories and made them more concrete. I hope that you also have been blessed.

REFERENCES

Akinyemi, Abayomi. 2008. *Avoid the Path to Pisgah*. Lake Mary, FL: Creation House, A Strang Company.

Baden-Powell, Robert. 1908. *Scouting for Boys*. Dover Publications.

Barth, Karl. 1977. *Dogmatik im Grundriß (Orig pub 1947)*. Zürich: Theologischer Verlag.

Bauer, Walter (BDAG). 2000. *A Greek-English Lexicon of the New Testament and Other Early Christian Literature*. 3rd ed. ed. de Frederick W. Danker. Chicago: University of Chicago Press. <BibleWorks. v. 9.>.

Bell, James Scott. 2014. *How to Write Dazzling Dialogue: The Fastest Way to Improve Any Manuscript*. Woodland Hills, CA: Compendium Press.

Benedict of Nursia, Saint. 2009. *The Holy Rule of St.* Benedict (Orig pub 547). Translated by Boniface Verheyen (1949), OSB of St. Benedict's Abbey, Atchison, Kansas (Kindle Edition).

BibleWorks. 2015. *Norfolk, VA: BibleWorks, LLC*. <BibleWorks v.10>.

Blackaby, Henry and Richard. 2002. *Hearing God's Voice*. Nashville: Broadman and Holman Publishers.

Bonhoeffer, Dietrich. 1954. *Life Together: The Classic Exploration of Christian Community (Gemeinsames Leben)*. Translated by John W. Doberstein. New York: HarperOne.

Bonhoeffer, Dietrich. 1995. *The Cost of Discipleship (Orig Pub 1937)*. Translated by R. H. Fuller and Irmgard Booth. New York: Simon & Schuster—A Touchstone Book.

Boyce, Mary. 2001. *Zoroastrians: Their Religious Beliefs and Practices*. New Yor: Routledge.

Bridge, William. 2003. *Managing Transitions: Making the Most of Change*. Cambridge: Da Capo Press.

Brooks, Larry. 2011. *Story Engineer: Mastering the Six Core Competencies of Successful Writing*. Cincinnati: Writer's Digest Books.

Brown-Driver-Briggs-Gesenius (BDB). 1905. *Hebrew-English Lexicon*. unabridged.

Card, Michael. 2005. *A Sacred Sorrow: Reaching Out to God in the Lost Language of Lament*. [Also: Experience Guide]. Colorado Springs: NavPress.

Carnegie, Dale. 1981. *How to Win Friends and Influence People (Orig pub 1936)*. New York: Simon and Schuster.

Chan, Simon. 1998. *Spiritual Theology: A Systematic Study of the Christian Life*. Downer's Grove, IL: IVP Academic.

Chandler, Jr. Alfred D. 1977. *The Visible Hand: The Managerial Revolution in American Business*. Cambridge: Harvard University Press; Belknap Press.

Clinebell, Howard J. Jr. 1978. *Understanding and Counseling the Alcoholic: Through Religion and Psychology*. Nashville: Abingdon.

Cloud, Henry and John Townsend. 1992. *Boundaries: When to Say YES; When to Say NO; To Take Control of Your Life*. Grand Rapids: Zondervan.

Cooper, Kenneth H. 1977. *The Aerobics Way*. New York: Bantam Books.

Coplien, James O. 1992. *Advanced C++ Programming Styles and Idioms*. Reading: Addison-Wesley Publishing Company.

DeCook, Stephen and JoAnn. 1999. *"DeKock, DeCook Ancestry."* July. Also manuscript *"The DeKock Group"* (both unpublished).

Dixon, Franklin W. 1959. *The Tower Treasure (The Hardy Boys No. 1; Orig Pub 1927)* Grosset & Dunlap.

Dreher, Rod. 2017. *The Benedict Option: A Strategy for Christians in a Post-Christian Nation*. New York: Sentinel.

Dürrenmatt, Friedrick. 1957. *Der Besuch der Alten Dame: Eine Tragische Komödie mit Einem Nachwort*. Edited by Paul Kurt Ackermann. Boston: Houghton Mifflin Company.

Faulkner, William. 2011. *A Fable (Orig Pub 1955)*. New York: Vintage International.

Foley, Michael P. [editor] 2006. *Augustine Confessions (Orig Pub 397 AD)*. 2nd Edition. Translated by F. J. Sheed (1942). Indianapolis: Hackett Publishing Company, Inc.

Foucault, Michel. 1988. *Madness and Civilization: A History of Insanity in the Age of Reason (Orig Pub 1965)*. Translated by Richard Howard. New York: Vintage Books.

Freeman, Philip. 2004. *Saint Patrick of Ireland: A Biography*. New York: Simon & Schuster.

Friedman, Edwin H. 1985. *Generation to Generation: Family Process in Church and Synagogue*. New York: Guilford Press.

General Assembly of the Presbyterian Church (U.S.A.). 1985. The Constitution of the Presbyterian Church (U.S.A.): Part II, Book of Order. New York.

Hellerman, Joseph H. 2001. *The Ancient Church as Family*. Minneapolis: Fortress Press.

Heschel, Abraham Joshua. 1951. *The Sabbath*. New York: Farrar, Straus, and Giroux.

Hiemstra, Stephen J. 2016a. *My Travel Through Life: Memoir of Family Life and Federal Service*. Centreville: T2Pneuma Publishers LLC.

Hiemstra, Stephen W. 1979. *Dual Market Structures in the Food Economy of Puerto Rico*. A Thesis. Cornell Unversity. January.

Hiemstra, Stephen W. 1980. *Selected Agricultural Statistics on Spain, 1965–76*. USDA. Economic Research Service (ERS). Statistical Bulletin 630. March.

Hiemstra, Stephen W. 1984. *"Technological and Organizational Changes in the U.S. Beef Packing Industry."* Office of Technological Assessment Working Paper. U.S. Congress. November.

Hiemstra, Stephen W. 1985a. *Labor Relations, Technological and Structural Change in U.S. Beef Packing and Retailing*. Dissertation for the Degree of PhD Michigan State University.

Hiemstra, Stephen W. 1985b. *"U.S. Share of World Rice Market Declines,"* Rice: Outlook and Situation. USDA. ERS. March.

Hiemstra, Stephen W. 1985c. *"U.S. Share of World Wheat Flour Market Declines,"* Wheat: Outlook and Situation. USDA. ERS. September.

Hiemstra, Stephen W. 1985d. *"U.S. Share of the World Wheat Market Declines,"* Wheat: Outlook and Situation. USDA. ERS. May.

Hiemstra, Stephen W. 1986. *"U.S. Farm Exports to EC Continue Falling,"* Foreign Agricultural Trade of the United States. USDA. ERS. November/December.

Hiemstra, Stephen W. and Arthur B. Mackie. 1986. *Methods of Reconciling World Trade Statistics.* USDA. ERS. Foreign Agricultural Economic Report (FAER) No. 217. May.

Hiemstra, Stephen W. 1987. *The Effect of Spain's Entry into the EC on the Demand for Imported Corn.* USDA. ERS. Staff paper No. AGES870916. October.

Hiemstra, Stephen W., and Stephen MacDonald. 1987. *Forecasting U.S. Agricultural Exports Using the Trade Estimates System.* USDA. ERS. Manuscript. May.

Hiemstra, Stephen W., and Mathew Shane. *Monetary Implications for GATT Agricultural Negotiations.* USDA. ERS. FAER No. 236. April 1988. (Revised reprint August 1988). 20 pp.

Hiemstra, Stephen W. 1991. *"Production and Use of Subject-Matter Research in the Federal Service: Example of Research on Farmer Mac," Agricultural Economics: The Journal of the International Association of Agricultural Economists.* July. pp. 237–251.

Hiemstra, Stephen W. 2009. *"Can Bad Culture Kill a Firm?" Risk Management.* Joint Risk Management Section, Society of Actuaries. 16: 51–54. June.

Hiemstra, Stephen W. 2010. *"Responding to Systemic Risk," Risk Management.* Joint Risk Management Section, Society of Actuaries. 20: 16–19. September.

Hiemstra, Stephen W. 2014. *A Christian Guide to Spirituality.* Centreville: T2Pneuma Publishers LLC.

Hiemstra, Stephen W. 2015. *Una Guía Cristiana a la Espiritualidad.* Centreville: T2Pneuma Publishers LLC.

Hiemstra, Stephen W. 2016b. *Life in Tension.* Centreville: T2Pneuma Publishers LLC.

Hiemstra, Stephen W. and Hyunok Lee. *1989. "Implications of Land Transfer Survey Data on Agricultural Mortgages for Farmer Mac,"* Presentation at the American Agricultural Economics Association summer meetings in Baton Rouge. August.

Hiemstra, Stephen W., Steven R. *Koenig*, and David Freshwater. 1988. *Prospects for a Secondary Market in Farm Mortgages.* USDA. ERS. Agricultural Economics Report No. 603. December. (Reprinted March 1989).

Hunter III, George G. 2000. *The Celtic Way of Evangelism: How Christianity can Reach the West . . .* Again. Nashville: Abingdon Press.

Hutcheson, Jr. Richard G. 1988. *God in the White House: How Religion Has Changed the Modern Presidency.* New York: MacMillan Publishing Company.

Hayasaki, Erika. 2016. *"Traces of Times Lost: How childhood memories shape us, even after we've forgotten them."* The Atlantic. November 29.

Icenogle, Garth Weldon. 1994. *Biblical Foundations for Small Group Ministry: An Integrational Approach.* Downers Grove: InterVarsity Press.

Iowa State University. 1977. *Proceedings of the World Food Conference of 1976, June 27–July 1.* Ames: Iowa State University Press.

Johnson, Glenn L. and C. Leroy Guance [editors]. 1972. *The Overproduction Trap in U.S. Agriculture: A Study of Resource Allocation from World War I to the Late 1960's*. Baltimore: Johns Hopkins University Press.

Johnson, Glenn L. 1986. *Research Methodology for Economists: Philosophy and Practice*. New York: Macmillan Publishing Company.

Karr, Mary. 2015. *The Art of Memoir*. New York: Harper Perennial.

King, Stephen. 2010. *On Writing: A Memoir of the Craft*. New York: Scribner.

Kreeft, Peter. 2007. *The Philosophy of Jesus*. South Bend, IN: Saint Augustine's Press.

Marx, Karl. 1887. *Capital A Critique of Political Economy: Volume I Book One: The Process of Production of Capital*. Edited by Frederick Engels; Translated by Samuel Moore and Edward Aveling. Moscow: Progress Publishers. Cited: 11 November 2016. Online: https://www.marxists.org/archive/marx/works/1867-c1.

Meadows, Donella, H. Dennis L. *Meadows, Jorgen Randers, and William W.* Behrens III. 1975. The Limits to Growth: A Report for the Club of Rome's Project on the Predicament of Mankind. New York: Universe Books Publishers.

Molley, John T. 1988. *New Dress for Success*. New York: Warner Books.

Moore, L.E. *1943*. *Elementary Aviation*. Boston: D.C. Heath and Company.

Nader, Ralph. 1965. *Unsafe at Any Speed: The Designed-in Dangers of the American Automobile*. New York: Grossman Publishers.

Nader, Ralph. 1971. *Action for a Change: A Student's Manual for Public Interest Organizing*. New York: Grossman Publishers.

Niebuhr, H. Richard. *1937*. *The Kingdom of God in America*. New York: Harper Torchbooks.

Ortberg, John. 2015. *All the Places to Go: How Will You Know? Carol Stream: Tyndale House Publishers*.

Patterson, Kerry. Joseph Grenny, Ron McMillan, and Al Switzler. *2012*. Crucial Conversations: Tools for Talking When Stakes Are High. New York: McGraw-Hill.

Peace, Richard. 1998. *Spiritual Autobiography: Discovering and Sharing Your Spiritual Story*. Colorado Springs: NavPress.

Peterson, Eugene H. 2006. *Eat This Book: A Conversation in the Art of Spiritual Reading*. Grand Rapids: Eerdmans.

Sacks, Jonah. 2012. *Winning the Story Wars: Why Those Who Tell—and Live—the Best Stories Will Rule the Future.* Boston: Harvard Business School Press.

Sahajwala, Ranjana and Paul Van den Bergh. 2000. *Supervisory Risk Assessment and Early Warning Systems, Bank for International Settlements (BIS), Basel, Switzerland Working Paper No 4, December.* Online: http://www.bis.org/publ/bcbs_wp4.pdf.

Sanders, J. Oswald. 1994. *Spiritual Leadership: Principles of Excellence for Every Believer.* Chicago: Moody Press.

Savage, John. 1996. *Listening & Caring Skills: A Guide for Groups and Leaders.* Nashville: Abingdon Press.

Sherrick, B.J., *Paul N.* Ellinger, Peter J. Barry, and A. D. Jacob. 2001. *FMAC Risk Based Capital Stress Test Model.* Model used to establish the Risk-Based capital requirement for the Federal Agricultural Mortgage Corporation.

Silverman, Sue William. 2009. *Fearless Confessions: A Writer's Guide to Memoir.* Athens: University of Georgia Press.

Skinner, B.F. 1971. *Beyond Freedom and Dignity.* New York: Bantam Books/Vintage Books.

Smith, Marion Roach. 2011. *The Memoir Project: A Thoroughly Non-Standardized Text for Writing and Life*. New York: Grand Central Publishing.

Sproul, R.C. *1982*. Reason to Believe: A Response to Common Objectives to Christianity. Grand Rapids: Zondervan.

Stanley, Andy and Lane Jones. 2006. *Communicating for a Change*. Colorado Springs: Multinomah Books.

Stanton, Thomas H. 2002. *Government Sponsored Enterprises: Mercantile Companies in the Modern World*. Washington D.C.: AEI Press.

Striker, Fran. 1936. *The Lone Ranger*. Sampson Low.

Stroustrup, Bjarne. 1991. *The C++ Programming Language*. Reading: Addison-Wesley Publishing Company.

Strunk, Jr. William, and E. B. White. 1979. *The Elements of Style*. New York: MacMillan Publishing Company, Inc.

Swamy, P. A. *V*. B. Thomas J. Lutton and Philip F. Bartholomew. 2001. *"Improved Methods of Treating Critical Issues in Regulating and Supervising Bank Safety and Soundness."* Research in Finance. Vol. 18:2000, 1–45.

Swanson, Ana. 2015. *"144 years of marriage and divorce in the United States, in one chart."* Washington Post. June 23. Online: http://wapo.st/1HaDGtW?tid=ss_mail.

Thoreau, Henry David. 1965. *Walden and Civil Disobedience.* New York: Harper and Row Publishers (Harper Classic).

Vanhoozer, Kevin, J. 2014. *Faith Speaking Understanding: Performing the Drama of Doctrine.* Louisville: Westminster John Knox Press.

Warren, Susan May. 2016. *The Story Equation.* Minneapolis: My Book Therapy.

Wilkerson, David. 1962. *The Cross and the Switchblade.* Pyramid Communications.

Williams, Joseph M. 2003. *Style: Ten Lessons in Clarity and Grace.* New York: Longman.

Wynne, John J. 2013. *The Jesuit Martyrs of North America (Orig Pub 1925 by Universal Knowledge Foundation).* Literary Licensing, LLC.

ABOUT THE AUTHOR

*A*uthor Stephen W. Hiemstra lives in Centreville, VA with Maryam, his wife of more than thirty years. Together, they have three grown children.

Stephen worked as an economist for twenty-seven years in more than five federal agencies, where he published numerous government studies, magazine articles, and book reviews. He wrote his first book, *A Christian Guide to Spirituality* in 2014. In 2015, he translated and published a Spanish edition, *Una Guía Cristiana a la Espiritualidad.* In 2016, he wrote a second book, *Life in Tension,* which also focuses on Christian spirituality.

Stephen has a Masters of Divinity (MDiv, 2013) from Gordon-Conwell Theological Seminary in Charlotte, NC. His doctorate (PhD, 1985) is in agricultural economics from Michigan State. He studied in Puerto Rico and Germany, and speaks Spanish and German.

Correspond with Stephen at T2Pneuma@gmail.com or follow his blog at http://www.T2Pneuma.net.